KESTREL SQUADRON
Groundcrew Memoirs

Brian Carlin

A former member of the groundcrew recalls his service with the VSTOL Tripartite Kestrel Evaluation Squadron

Copyright © 2017 Brian Carlin
Cover design and art © 2017 Brian Carlin

ISBN: 9781521246924

All rights reserved, including the right to reproduce this book or portions thereof in any form whatsoever.
For information or permissions, please contact the author.
Email address: **brian.carlin29@gmail.com**

Published by Brian Carlin

KESTREL SQUADRON

Also by Brian Carlin

Boy Entrant

Dedicated to those who served on, or supported the Tripartite Kestrel Evaluation Squadron at RAF Station West Raynham, Norfolk, England during the squadron's existence, 1964 to 1966.

TABLE OF CONTENTS

Foreword xi

Acknowledgements xiii

Introduction xv

Chapter 1: Early Days 1

Chapter 2: Tripartite 7

Chapter 3: Dunsfold 15

Chapter 4: Kestrels Arrive 21

Chapter 5: Personal Transportation Ups and Downs 29

Chapter 6: Disaster on Day One 35

Chapter 7: Ubendum and Webendum 47

Chapter 8: Working with the Americans 69

Chapter 9: A Hurricane and Another Kind of Kestrel 87

Chapter 10: The Squadron Disbands 93

Chapter 11: Kestrel Squadron Aftermath 99

Chapter 12: The Fate of the Aircraft 115

Chapter 13: About the Author 127

Appendix: Kestrel Squadron Nominal Roll 131

Foreword

My intent in writing this book is to provide a glimpse of what it was like to be a member of a very unique military unit, the Tripartite Kestrel Evaluation Squadron, albeit from the relatively unglamorous point of view of a groundcrew member. I try to give the reader a feel for the behind the scenes operations, what it was like to work in close concert with military personnel from other nations, an insight into the nuts and bolts of the Kestrel evaluation trials and commentary on some of the personalities involved.

The book also chronicles the eventual fate of the Kestrels after the work of the squadron was complete. Several of the aircraft still survive to the present day and are, for the most part, in good hands.

At the time of the evaluation, I was a young, junior-ranking, non-commissioned RAF member with no previous experience of interacting with citizens of other nations. On the squadron, most of these were Americans. Although such naïveté is akin to water that has long passed under the bridge, I have tried to get back into the head of my younger self to relate my then impressions of those others. Ironically, in later life and arising from different circumstances, I too became an American citizen, which goes to show how strange life's journey can somehow turn out to be.

My time spent on the squadron is also a part of my personal life history and therefore diverges on occasions from the main subject matter. I hope you can forgive this indulgence and even find it a little interesting.

Brian Carlin
San Diego, California
May 2017

Acknowledgements

The content of this book is derived not only from personal recollections but also, in no small part, from contributions by former Kestrel Squadron colleagues.

Captain Jim Tyson USN (retired) graciously provided some of anecdotes and an in-depth account of the U.S. Navy trials of the Kestrel in the United States following the Tripartite Kestrel Evaluation Squadron trials at RAF West Raynham.

My gratitude also to Charles "Chuck" Massey (USAF, retired) for the information that he imparted during our several phone conversations and for the documents and photographs he so generously provided.

Many of the photographs, especially of squadron operations, are provided thanks to Günter Findiesen's presence of mind in bringing his camera to work and my heartfelt gratitude to his wife Beryl for passing them on via Bonny Boniface.

Speaking of Bonny Boniface, my grateful thanks to him for soliciting the abovementioned photos and providing some of his own, and for his anecdotes of some of the events that occurred during squadron operations. He and I enjoyed a memorable reunion 50 years after the event when we arranged a joint visit to Newark Air Museum in Nottinghamshire, England.

My friend Sheila Roberts helped tremendously by agreeing to proof read my work, catching the grammatical errors, missed out words and making sound suggestions in phrasing. Therefore, to Sheila, I offer a grateful thank you.

I would also like to thank my friend Bruce Allen for obligingly taking pictures of the Harrier display at the 2015 Miramar Airshow, one of which appears early in the book.

Introduction

Military air shows are one of today's great crowd-pleasing spectacles. Who among us has not experienced an adrenaline rush brought on by the high-speed, low-level pass of a high performance jet aircraft as it screams through the viewing area? Or has not been awestruck by elegant aerial ballets performed in the vast vault of the sky by precision aerobatic teams like the Red Arrows or Blue Angels?

It would be impossible for me to count the number of such shows I have attended over the years, on both sides of the Atlantic. For many of those years, and right up to the present time, one of the great air show favourites has always been the Harrier demonstrating its unique VSTOL capabilities. The display usually ends with the aircraft hovering for a few minutes in front of the viewing area, moving slowly backwards and forwards, turning in slow circles, finally bowing gracefully to spectators before noisily transitioning to forward flight and then departing the display area. The crowds have always loved it and applaud wildly. I too applaud, but also experience a fleeting moment of smugness because the demonstration is no novelty to me. You see, I share some of this aircraft's early history – a history that goes back some fifty or so years. To be more precise, the history I share is with its predecessor and direct ancestor, the Hawker Siddeley Kestrel. This while serving as an electrical technician groundcrew member on the Tripartite Kestrel Evaluation Squadron at RAF Station West Raynham from 1964 until 1966

The Tripartite Kestrel Evaluation Squadron was founded on 15th of October 1964 for the sole purpose of evaluating the military application of a VSTOL jet fighter aircraft, but the squadron had its genesis somewhat earlier with development of the Hawker Siddeley VSTOL (Vertical Short Takeoff and Landing) aircraft known as the P1127. Although initially it was a privately funded Hawker Siddeley design, the British, American and West German governments shared later development costs.

Around this same time, NATO was experimenting with a concept known as the Multi Lateral Force (MLF). This had been an idea kicked around during the administrations of three American presidents: Eisenhower, Kennedy, and Johnson. The most well known example of the MLF was the manning of the *USS Claude V. Ricketts* by a multi-national crew. The Tripartite Kestrel Evaluation Squadron was formed with the same concept in mind, and termed "tripartite" because squadron personnel were envisaged to consist, in equal numbers, of British, American and West German service members.

The squadron formation began in 1963, when a group of pilots representing each of the three nations came together in Britain to develop an evaluation protocol. These officers were Wing Commander Scrimgeour (the proposed squadron's commanding officer), RAF; Lieutenant Colonel Solt, US Army; Commander Tyson, US Navy; Major Campbell, USAF, and Oberst (Colonel) Barkhorn, German Air Force. A workable plan emerged from this *téte-a-téte*, together with a firm decision to form the evaluation squadron in October of the following year and base it at RAF West Raynham, in Norfolk, England.

INTRODUCTION

xvii

A US Marine Corps AV-8B Harrier demonstrates its hovering ability during the Marine Corps Air Station Miramar Air Show in October 2015.
(Photo by Bruce Allen)

Chapter 1: *Early Days*

Although the P1127 VSTOL aircraft received periodic mentions in the news at the time, I was unaware of any plans for the formation of an international squadron to evaluate the VSTOL concept and never dreamt for a moment that I would be associated with it in any way. In fact, for me, the most important event of 1964 was getting married to my fiancée Pam in June that year. However, as it turned out, the second most important event of that same year came later, when I was unexpectedly posted to the unique Tripartite Kestrel Evaluation Squadron.

At that time, I was a Junior Technician (J/T) Electrical Fitter on the Vulcan aircraft Flight Line Squadron at RAF Waddington, working alternate weeks of days and nights and the occasional stint on Swing Shift (midnight to 8 am). Being of junior rank, with no children and not many years service, I had nowhere near enough points to qualify for housing in married quarters, so like most other young newlyweds in the service, my bride and I had rented a furnished flat in the city of Lincoln.

Commuting backwards and forwards to Waddington from the opposite side of Lincoln, where our flat was located, called for some means of transportation, and to meet this need I had purchased a somewhat ancient Lambretta motor scooter from one of the corporals on my shift.

After our honeymoon, life had settled into a new routine of daily and nightly journeys on the Lambretta, during which I was often forced to dismount because the spark plug had a tendency to "whisker up" due to the oil in the scooter's two-stroke engine fuel mixture. Chas, the corporal from whom I bought the scooter, had warned me about this, pointing out a little compartment under the seat containing a box spanner and wire brush. These would be needed when the power fell off and the engine began to misfire, both telltale signs of the need to de-whisker. So, week in, week out, I made the trip to and from Waddington in what soon became the cosy routine of my new, married life.

However, the RAF often came up with ways that could quickly upset one's cosy routine. The first inkling of my upcoming association with the Kestrel came one day in early October when I arrived for work. Within minutes of alighting from the bus that conveyed my shift from the Waddington domestic site out to flight line, the squadron "discip" sergeant pulled two of us aside; both of us J/T electricians. He then informed us that we were being posted to another station and told us to report to Station Headquarters (SHQ) right away. There, we learned that the posting was to the Kestrel Evaluation Squadron at RAF West Raynham in Norfolk.

The SHQ clerk informed us it was a "tripartite" squadron, and that we would be working in concert with American and West German servicemen to evaluate the Hawker Siddeley P1127 VSTOL aircraft. The official date of our posting was 15th of October 1964, which was about one week hence.

The prospect of being in the forefront of a new type of aircraft, and to be working with personnel from other nations filled me with excitement. However, the other J/T managed to talk his way out of the posting because he had recently purchased a house in Lincoln, which he and his wife did not want to leave. No one else from Waddington filled his place, so within a few days I set off alone, on Wednesday, 14th of October, with orders to report to my new squadron at RAF West Raynham. To enable me to travel home to Lincoln at weekends, I decided to make the 80-mile journey to West Raynham on my marginally trusty Lambretta. Other than the customary stops every few miles to clean the spark plug, I managed to get there safely by mid afternoon that day.

After I had signed in at the guardroom and collected some bedding from the Bedding Store, the duty Service Police corporal directed me to a billet assigned to the squadron. Several other new squadron members had already arrived, so introductions were made all around as I dumped my kit on one of the still available beds, at the same time hoping that this demotion to bachelor life was only temporary, having enjoyed the happy state of married life for just a mere four months.

EARLY DAYS

The next day, as part of the usual RAF "Arrival" process, those of us housed in the billet reported to the Squadron Orderly Room at the hangar from where we would be operating. This hangar, on the end of a row of four identical hangars, had taken some punishment during the Second World War when Luftwaffe aircraft regularly strafed the airfield. Several bullet holes pock-marked the hangar door structural steel supports and there was a large hole high up on the brickwork where a round of cannon fire had made an impressionable impact. Later, tongue-in-cheek, a few of us ribbed members of the German contingent about this damage, but at this juncture there were neither Germans nor aircraft on the squadron, and only one US Army sergeant; a clerk who worked in the squadron office. Without aircraft, there was little to do except sit in the crew-room and get to know the other lads, although there were occasional interruptions by one or other of the SNCOs popping in to assign irritating, keep-busy tasks, such as hangar floor sweeping or moving equipment around.

Fortunately, because of my electrical trade, they assigned me to help the squadron store-men with the mammoth task of etching identifying marks on the squadron hand tools. For safety reasons, tools used for aircraft maintenance were retained on a large "shadow board" in the store, and were loaned out to individuals on an as-needed basis. Each tool had a unique serial number, which the borrower recorded on a sign-out form so that the store-men could keep track of the tools to help ensure that none was accidentally left in an aircraft. At the end of the working day, he could tell at a glance whether all tools were back on the shadow board. The Kestrel Squadron tools were brand new, so their assigned serial numbers needed to be etched onto a metal part of the tool, using an electric etching tool. In this way, the tool's serial number could be applied indelibly. Military logic, such as it is, reasoned that since the etching tool was an electrical device, an electrician was the most suitably qualified person to operate it, which is why I was given the assignment. Store-man Dave King and I worked at this task for several days and, in the process, struck up a firm friendship, often getting together socially, accompanied by our wives, throughout our time on the squadron.

***

That first weekend, I headed back to Lincoln on the scooter to spend a couple of days with Pam, who had moved back into her parents' home. In doing so, however, I missed out on a great adventure. There was a film crew shooting location scenes at the nearby small seaside town of Wells-next-the-Sea for the film, *"Operation Crossbow."* This film dramatised a real wartime operation of the same name that struck against the German V1 and V2 rocket development projects. Representatives of the film company visited the station over the weekend looking for extras and, since most of the Kestrel Squadron lads had stayed there, they all volunteered. I found out about it on returning to the camp on Sunday night. The location on the beach at Wells-next-the-Sea doubled as Peenemunde, where the V-1 was developed. The scene they were shooting portrayed German aviator Hanna Reitsch piloting a V-1 "doodle bug" to trouble-shoot a controls problem that the rocket had been experiencing up to that time. Our squadron lads were outfitted in German uniforms and directed to move around the location background while the main filming was going on. One pair even got to ride around in a motor cycle/sidecar combination. I was sorry to have missed it all, but spending a couple of days with my wife was much more rewarding.

During the following week, word came from the Orderly Room that married quarters would be provided at nearby RAF Sculthorpe for all other-ranks married personnel. Sculthorpe had been a recent USAF Strategic Air Command (SAC) base, but was currently unoccupied. The officers would be provided with housing appropriate to their rank on the disused RAF Bircham Newton base.

In addition to the traditional RAF-style married quarters at Sculthorpe, there were also twice as many single storey bungalow-style houses that were completely unlike the standard RAF type of married quarter housing. These bungalows were nicknamed "tobacco houses" because the Americans had paid the British government in tobacco instead of cash to have them built when the USAF occupied the base. Besides being single storey, the tobacco houses were equipped with central heating, also unlike traditional RAF married quarters that relied on coal fires and coke burning stoves for heating. The plan was to house RAF personnel in the traditional quarters, while the Americans would be accommodated in the tobacco houses.

EARLY DAYS

Pam and I "marched in" to our new married quarter on a foggy afternoon in early November. There was no actual marching involved. The term was supposedly a hangover from earlier times, when there was some ceremony involved, during which the new occupant would be literally marched into the house along with his wife and children. We just went around with a representative of the Families Section to inspect the house and note anything that was not up to par. There was not much to note because the house was equipped with brand new furniture and all the necessities needed to set up home, from teaspoons to tablecloths. This was a godsend because we really had very little of our own stuff. One of Pam's relatives had driven us there from Lincoln, together with our sole possessions – a single tub Hoover washing machine equipped with a manually operated wringer, a coffee table, and our personal clothing, all of which, including ourselves, fitted into his beat up Bedford van. We had brought a few items of food but no fresh milk or bread, so resigned ourselves to the fact that we would have to find some shops in the nearby village next morning before we could have anything to eat. That was if the thick fog, which had descended during the evening, lifted sufficiently for us to find our way there. However, there was a pleasant surprise in store for us. Early next morning, we awoke to the sound of something plopping through the letterbox. Going downstairs, I discovered that morning's edition of *The Daily Mirror* on the hallway floor and a bottle of milk on the doorstep. We had no idea as to the identity of our benefactor, but later that day there was a polite knock at the door. We opened it to find a beaming tradesman standing on the doorstep. He was dressed in white smock over which he wore a traditional butcher's blue striped apron. Behind him, we could see a van parked at the kerb. In his quaint Norfolk accent, he introduced himself as the village butcher, cum milkman, cum newsagent. We immediately opened an account with him, and every day thereafter, he delivered milk and a newspaper to our door first thing in the morning. Later in the day, he came with a selection of meats, which he cut to order on a butcher's block in the rear of his van. A baker and grocer also made the rounds of married quarters in their vans so we were not without the basics of life right from the very first day.

Those of us moving into married quarters were given a few days off to get ourselves settled in. Not having too much stuff of our own, the settling-in didn't take Pam and me very long, so we had some free time to explore our surroundings. One particular day, we hopped on the motor scooter to look around the large, deserted camp and, on turning a corner in an area that held nothing more than a few derelict, partially demolished wooden buildings, we unexpectedly came upon a film crew. They were in the middle of shooting a scene that featured an elegantly dressed gentleman wearing a bowler hat and carrying a neatly furled umbrella. He was standing in the remains of one of the ruined buildings, gazing intently at something that we couldn't actually see. Being dedicated fans of *The Avengers* television series, we immediately recognised the gentleman as the late Patrick McNee, known as John Steed in the series, so we stopped to watch. However, my noisy scooter engine must have interrupted the shot because an evidently irritated member of the crew gestured impatiently for us to move on, which we obligingly did. But at least we got a glimpse of Mr. McNee in the flesh. Some months later, when the first "*Avengers*" episode of the 1965 season aired, it included the scene we had briefly witnessed being shot. The episode's title is "*The Town of No Return*," which can still be found and viewed on the Internet. It is also the episode in which Diana Rigg made her debut in the series as Emma Peel.

Shortly after having moved into our married quarter, we noticed that a few Americans had taken up residence in the tobacco houses. Three of them took regular walks past our house on Lancaster Road. All three wore US Navy uniforms – two in petty officer uniforms, and the third in a traditional USN white sailor's cap. Neither side attempted to contact the other although later on I came to know all three very well.

Chapter 2: Tripartite

The remainder of the US contingent began trickling in during the next few days, although the German Air Force (GAF) contingent still had not shown up. The intention was to operate the squadron with approximately 120 personnel, split between the three nations, theoretically providing 40 officers and men from each. However, at some juncture between the original political agreement and the establishment of the squadron, the West German government became lukewarm about its involvement. Consequently, it decided to contribute only a token force of six personnel to the squadron consisting of three officers and three NCOs. In order to make up the shortfall, the RAF had agreed to provide the balance of personnel. In the end, the squadron strength rounded out at 128 officers and men, consisting of 82 RAF personnel and 40 Americans, the latter consisting of personnel from the US Navy, the US Army and the US Air Force. The Germans made up the balance of six.

With the arrival of the US and German contingents, the squadron came up to full strength under the leadership of RAF Wing Commander David Scrimgeour. However, although RAF personnel outnumbered everyone else, since most of the Americans were senior NCOs, they took on the leadership role of the "other ranks" (or enlisted) personnel. The hangar "boss" was a US Army Master Sergeant (M/Sgt.) named Jones and my particular domain, the Electrical & Instrument (E&I) Section, was ruled by US Navy Senior Chief Petty Officer (SCPO) Roby. Roby was one of the three USN men we had noticed taking walks around the married quarters at Sculthorpe, (it turned out that the other two were Chief Petty Officer Chester Mouton and Petty Officer/2 Angelo Lucero – the latter being the wearer of the traditional USN sailor cap).

Two of the three officers of the German contingent were pilots and the third was an engineering officer. The three German NCOs comprised two Feldwebels (equivalent to a RAF Sergeant) and one Stabsunteroffizier, a rank that has no direct RAF equivalent, but falls somewhere between our corporal and sergeant ranks. Small though it was, an interesting aspect of the German contingent was that its senior officer, Oberst Gerhard Barkhorn, (his rank equivalent to a Group Captain or army Colonel), was reputed to be the second highest scoring Luftwaffe fighter ace during the Second World War. His score during that conflict exceeded only by that of Erich Hartmann, although it was hastily claimed that Barkhorn's honours were all earned on the Russian Front. He had also flown sorties over England during the Battle of Britain, but had not been successful during that campaign. On the squadron, he was known as Colonel Barkhorn and was a very popular and approachable officer. The other German pilot was 1st Lieutenant Suhr, the youngest of all the pilots, and the Engineering Officer was Hauptman Duskow.

On the British side, in addition to Wing Commander Scrimgeour, (also a pilot), we had three other pilots, namely Squadron Leader Trowern, Flight Lieutenant "Porky" Munro, and Flight Lieutenant Edmonston. There were a few other non-aircrew officers and the usual assortment of "other ranks" from Warrant Officer all the way down to a Leading Aircraftsman (LAC).

The American pilots represented three of their services. Lieutenant Colonel Solt (later replaced by Major Curry) and Major Johnston were US Army pilots. Commander Tyson represented the US Navy, and Major Campbell was a USAF pilot. With the advantage of hindsight, it seems rather ironic that the US Marine Corps did not have a pilot on the squadron, yet it was the only US service to later adopt the VSTOL concept by equipping with the Harrier.

***

Before joining Kestrel Squadron my only knowledge of German people was through seeing them portrayed unrealistically in films or from the rare television appearances of real individuals. My first experience of actually meeting someone from Germany, in the flesh, happened in early November 1964 when Corporal John Ralphs (my next-door neighbour in married quarters) and I were "volunteered" to escort one of the GAF Feldwebels to the Hawker Siddeley factory at Dunsfold in Surrey, where he would be attending a Kestrel training course. The Feldwebel's name was Dieter (pronounced "Deetur") Zinndorf and he spoke only a few words of English. Since both John and I were also attending the same training course, those in authority obviously felt we could help Dieter navigate the trials and tribulations of British Railways and, just as importantly, assist him with being accommodated at RAF Odiham, where we would all be billeted for the duration of the two-week course.

On the Sunday morning of our journey to Odiham, a RAF "J2" minibus, driven by the duty MT driver, drew up outside our married quarters. Dieter was already on board, having been picked up from the West Raynham Sergeants Mess where he was billeted. Like John and me, he was dressed in civvies. The driver took us to Kings Lynn railway station, where we caught a train for London and, from there, made our way to Odiham by way of rail to Hook in Hampshire and then by RAF transport from the railway station to the camp. During the journey, John and I managed to communicate with our travelling companion in halting English and the few German words I remembered from my first-year German language lessons in grammar school. Dieter made frequent references to his German/English pocket dictionary, often asking us to point out an English word we had used so that he could see its German equivalent. This method of communication worked reasonably well for him, although he became noticeably less vocal when we were within earshot of anyone else.

An early darkness had fallen on the typically dank, dreary November day by the time we arrived at RAF Odiham. On signing in at the guardroom, we were each issued the usual bundle of bedding. Being a corporal, John was assigned a single room bunk, while Dieter Zinndorf and I were directed to the transit billet. I have rested my weary bones in many transit billets during my service, none of them ever the nicest of places to kip down, but this particular transit billet ranked at the bottom of the list as the most miserable one in which I had ever set foot. A row of large lockers walled off most of the barrack room and a single, naked light bulb illuminated the only small area available to us. The beds were configured as bunk beds and, to cap it all, several damp, off-white garments dangled from a makeshift clothesline that one of the existing occupants had strung diagonally across the middle of the space. This not only created the impression of a low-rent bed-sitter, but also put half the area into shadow by obstructing light from the single light bulb. My German companion took one look at this hellhole and firmly said "Nein!" Then, as best he could in his limited English, strongly conveyed to me that he was not staying there because he was equivalent in rank to a sergeant and should be accommodated with the SNCOs. I immediately felt sorry for him, understanding his desolation at being stuck in a foreign country with limited language skills and now expected to be billeted in this slum. At the same time, I was embarrassed for the service of which I was a representative.

Dumping my bedding on one of the vacant beds, I walked Dieter back to the guardroom and asked for the Orderly Sergeant. Having explained the situation to him, bolstered by the fact that my Feldwebel friend was billeted in the Sergeants Mess at West Raynham, we were both relieved when the Sergeant took charge of the situation and got Dieter booked into the Odiham Sergeants Mess. I said goodnight to Dieter before heading back to the "slum," where it was my unfortunate fate to reside for the next two weeks. Although unable to express himself well at the time, later, when he was much more fluent in English, Dieter thanked me for my efforts in getting him moved into the Sergeants Mess on that dreary evening. We had a good laugh as we recalled the ridiculousness of the situation in which we had both found ourselves and, over time, we became good friends.

Altogether, there were six RAF personnel attending courses - Chief Technician Jim Brookes, Corporal Clive Cox and I were on the electrical course, while Sergeant Don Grunwell, Corporal "Bonny" Boniface and Corporal John Ralphs were on the airframe course.

Chief Tech. Brookes and Sgt. Grunwell were accommodated in the Sergeants Mess with Dieter Zinndorf, while Bonny and Clive, like John Ralphs, were billeted in single-room Corporal bunks. Bonny had driven there in his car because he intended to go home for weekends. Chief Tech. Brookes also had a car, so all agreed we would commute to and from Dunsfold in these two cars and share the petrol costs. Don Grunwell and Dieter Zinndorf would travel with Jim Brookes, since they were all in the Sergeants Mess, while John, Clive and I would travel with Bonny.

The Americans on the training course had made other arrangements. There were five of them and they had been booked into a small private hotel in the area that, I am pretty sure, served much nicer breakfasts than those served up in the Odiham Airmen's Mess.

All twelve of us met up on the first day of the course. Both USN Senior Chief Petty Officer Roby and USAF Master Sergeant "Buck" Arbuckle were on the electrical course, while US Army Master Sergeant Jones and USAF Master Sergeant Bill Heim were in the airframes class, as was Dieter Zinndorf and USN PO/2 Angelo Lucero.

Apparently, the representatives of the three nations had been briefed on what to wear while taking the course. We RAF types had been instructed to dress in our working blue uniforms. The Americans, on the other hand, turned up in their best uniforms, while Dieter Zinndorf wore a civilian suit. Personally, I felt a bit scruffy dressed in my "hairy" working blue alongside the Yanks, but "orders is orders" as the saying goes.

The ten pilots who flew with the Kestrel Evaluation Squadron.
Back Row: Sqn Ldr Fred Trowern; Lt Col Lou Solt; Wg Cdr David Scrimgeour; Col Gerhard Barkhorn; Flt Lt David Edmondston.
Front Row: Capt Volke Suhr; Maj Al Johnson; Maj J K Campbell; Lt Cdr Jim Tyson; Flt Lt 'Porky' Munro.
(Photo courtesy of the Royal Air Force Historical Society)

Squadron members and instructors on the first Hawker Siddeley Kestrel training course. Back row, (L to R) Chief Instructor Mr. Holman; Instructor Pat Noyce, (Electrical Systems); Ch. Tech. Brookes; M/Sgt Jones; Cpl Boniface; Snr. Ch. P.O. Roby; M/Sgt Arbuckle; J/T Carlin (author); M/Sgt. Heims; Instructor Alf Black, (Airframes).
Front row, Feldwebel Zinndorf; Cpl. Ralphs; P.O.2 Lucero; Sgt. Grunwell; Cpl. Cox Instructor Mr. Anton.
(Photo courtesy of Hawker Siddeley Aviation from the author's personal collection)

Chapter 3: Dunsfold

The first week of the course was a general overview of the Kestrel aircraft during which, amongst other things, we learned how the VSTOL (Vertical, Short Take Off and Landing) concept worked. Cold air from the low pressure compressor stage of the Pegasus 5 engine discharged through the front rotatable nozzles while the rear nozzles ducted the hot jet exhaust after the air and fuel had mixed and ignited in the combustion chamber. Also, at very low airspeeds, when a Kestrel was operating in VSTOL mode, there would be insufficient air passing over the control surfaces for effective directional control. To provide these control functions in this mode, small variable aperture air ducts – "puffer jets" – were positioned at the wing tips, at the nose and tail, and on either side of the aft end of the fuselage to send a reactive discharge of air that had the same effect as its corresponding control surface. The puffer jets – or Reaction Controls, to give them their proper name – were controlled by the same control column and rudder pedals that operated the control surfaces in conventional flight. The air for the jets was bled off from the high pressure compressor. Although this air was bled off upstream of the combustion chamber, it was still very hot due to it being compressed.

We were also instructed in the handling procedures relating to the aircraft and the safety precautions that needed to be observed while performing servicing tasks. For example, we learned that the entire wing section was a single, contiguous element that sat atop the aircraft and was held in place by four stout bolts. This facilitated the easy dismantling of the aircraft into two main components – fuselage and wing section – for easy loading onto a "Queen Mary" transporter if the Kestrel became unfit to fly from a remote location.

The ejection seat was a particularly interesting feature. Prior to the Kestrel, ejection seats were designed for operation at altitudes and airspeeds typical of conventional types of jet aircraft. Those seats travelled approximately 120 feet vertically out of the cockpit after the slipstream had whisked the jettisoned canopy safely clear of the aircraft. However, these features were unsuitable for safe ejection from the VSTOL Kestrel. If an ejection were necessary when flying at a very low airspeed, or hovering close to the ground, the standard seat would not travel high enough for the parachute to develop fully. What's more, the jettisoned canopy would remain within the immediate area of the cockpit, resulting in a probable collision with the seat as it left the aircraft. Martin Baker overcame the vertical travel problem by adding a rocket pack to the underside of the seat, which shot it to 300 feet on ejection. Also, the Kestrel's large bubble canopy was not jettisoned. Instead, the top part of the seat simply smashed through it. (The later Harrier canopy incorporated an explosive ribbon to shatter the canopy in a fraction of a second before the seat ejected, but the Kestrel did not possess this refinement). Thus, the Kestrel became one of the first aircraft to be equipped with the Martin Baker Mk 6HA "zero-zero" ejection seat – suitable for ejection at zero altitude and zero airspeed.

During that first week, the training course group toured the factory production line. In addition to seeing some of the squadron's Kestrels in their various stages of production, we were also taken to an area of the production floor where a Second World War vintage Hawker Hurricane was being refurbished. Our guide was very proud of the work being done and informed us that this particular aircraft was the very last Hurricane ever built. To emphasise his point, the legend *"The Last of Many"* was neatly lettered along both sides of the fuselage. As it turned out, we were to see more of this famous aircraft at a later date.

The second week of the course saw us break into two separate trade-specific classes – electrical and airframes. I was in the electrical group, together with Jim Brookes, SCPO Roby, Clive Cox and USAF Master Sergeant "Buck" Arbuckle, all of us being taught the intricacies and components of the Kestrel electrical system by a congenial instructor named Pat Noyce. At the end of the course, we all received a certificate of completion that pronounced us qualified to service the world's first successful VSTOL aircraft.

During this period and for the following few months, other trades also attended training courses. The Engine fitters went to the Bristol Siddeley factory at Filton (Bristol Siddeley later became Rolls Royce), the Armourers' course was at Martin Baker's Denham facility and the Instrument fitters attended their course at Sperry's in Brentford.

The pilots also attended an engine course at Filton and a Kestrel ground course at Dunsfold, followed by conversion training on the aircraft. Those pilots who were experienced only in the handling of fast jet aircraft were also provided with a few hours of helicopter flying experience to familiarise themselves with experience of vertical and vectored flight.

Most of Britain experienced a White Christmas in 1964. A meteorological report from that time reads, "During the rather cold month of December, snow or sleet fell…daily in England and Wales…from the 25th until the end of the month." January saw more of the same white stuff. "Snow lay 2 – 4 inches deep in many parts of the Midlands and northern and eastern England." This made travel on the small roads and lanes around Sculthorpe and West Raynham challenging, but as the old saying goes, 'It's an ill wind that blows nobody any good.' The boffins saw an opportunity, courtesy of the substantial snow-cover, to test how the Kestrel could taxi in severe winter conditions. Since the squadron had still not received any of its aircraft, one of the Hawker Siddeley test pilots flew a Kestrel up from Dunsfold so that the trial could take place at West Raynham. A helicopter was needed not only to monitor and film the operation, but also to be available to rescue the pilot if the Kestrel became mired in the snow out in a remote part of the airfield. For reasons unknown, a Royal Navy Whirlwind chopper was assigned to perform this task, even though the RAF had helicopters capable of doing the job, as did the US Army.

The Kestrel performed well in the snow, but when it returned to the hangar, the groundcrew found that snow had accumulated in the wheel bay and was packed in there so solidly that it couldn't be removed without causing damage to local equipment and the aircraft structure. They decided to leave things as they were and just parked the Kestrel in the hangar overnight, letting nature take its course. In the morning, as expected, there was a large puddle of water on the floor that the hangar crew needed to mop up, but otherwise the Kestrel was unharmed and returned to Dunsfold that day.

18   KESTREL SQUADRON

Squadron members and instructors on Hawker Siddeley Kestrel training courses. Back row (L to R), H.S. Chief Instructor Mr. Holman; P.O.2 Staffanson; W.O. Grover; Snr. M/Sgt. Prines; Cpl Boniface; M/Sgt Jones; Mjr. King; Stuffz. Scheding; Hauptman Duskow; M/Sgt. Heims; H.S. Instructors Mr. Anton and Mr. Alf Black. Front row (L to R), Cpl. Ralphs; W.O. Grover; P.O.2 Lucero; Sgt. Grunwell; Cpl. May; Feldwebels Zinndorf and Findiesen.
(Photo courtesy of Hawker Siddeley Aviation via Bonny Boniface)

Squadron members and instructors on the second Kestrel training course at Dunsfold. Back row: (L to R) Cpl. Oliver; M/Sgt. Dix; Staff Sgt. Snyder; Sgt Smith; CPO Lynn. Front row: Tech./Sgt Massey; P.O.2 Osbourn; W.O. Grover; Mjr. King; J/T Thornley; Chief Instructor Mr. Holman; Instructor Pat Noyce, (Electrical Systems).
(Photo courtesy of Hawker Siddeley Aviation via Chuck Massey)

20   KESTREL SQUADRON

A Bristol Siddeley engine training course instructor points out features of the Pegasus 5 engine to squadron members (L to R) Feldwebel Findiesen; Instructor (unnamed); Chief Tech. Burrows; Flt. Sgt. Angel; W.O. Grover; P.O.2 Staffanson; Stuffz. Scheding; Snr. M/Sgt. Prines; Cpl. May; Sqdn. Ldr. Burke; Mjr. King; Hauptman Duskow.
(Photo courtesy of Bristol Siddeley via Chuck Massey)

Chapter 4: Kestrels Arrive

Ironically, the first aircraft delivered to the squadron was not a Kestrel but a De Havilland Beaver that the US Army had loaned to the squadron for general use. It arrived in early December.

The first Kestrel to arrive at West Raynham was XS694, on February 8, 1965. One of the squadron pilots flew it from Dunsfold on completion of his conversion training. On each wing, the aircraft bore the unique roundel designed especially for the squadron. It consisted of three pie shaped segments. The familiar RAF roundel occupied the upper (or forward, with respect to the direction of travel) segment. The two other segments occupied the lower left and right "pie slices" and were based on the insignias and national flag colours of the Federal Republic of Germany and the USA, respectively.

The tailfin bore nine, narrow vertical bars representing all three national flag colours; black, red and yellow for Germany and two sets of red, white and blue. One of these, with a slightly lighter blue bar, was for the USA and the set with the darker blue bar represented Britain. The representation of the German colours was puzzling because of the vertical nature of the bars, which seemed more representative of the Belgian national flag than the horizontal bars of Germany's flag, but it seems artistic licence or convenience trumped accuracy. Later, a large numeral "4" was painted on both sides of the nose of the aircraft, just forward of the cockpit. This was the last digit of the aircraft registration number. Similar derived numbers would adorn all the other Kestrels, making identification of the individual aircraft easier, although the number 0 on the nose of XS690, delivered much later, always seemed a little odd to me.

From then on, it was commonplace to hear the loud whoosh of a Kestrel engine's cartridge start system operating and see the thick, dark plume of smoke that was expelled upwards as it vented from the starter exhaust located just behind the cockpit canopy. The whooshing sound and the smoke resulted from the firing of a large brass cartridge similar in size and appearance to a howitzer shell, except that the projectile part was missing. In other words, it was a "blank." When fired electrically, the explosive force of the gases bursting out of the cartridge rotated a small turbine at a high speed. The small turbine then engaged with the engine, through a gearing system, to bring the engine rapidly up to starting speed. At the same time, fuel fed to the engine combustion chamber was ignited by a high-energy electrical spark plug, enabling the engine to accelerate to self-sustaining speed.

The cartridge start system endowed the Kestrel with complete independence from any kind of engine-starting ground equipment. This meant that a pilot could start the engine anywhere, regardless of whether he was at his home base, or at the most primitive of forward bases – those for which the aircraft was designed to operate. Two starter cartridges were always loaded into the system's twin-chambered breech during each pre-flight preparation. One cartridge was expended during the first engine start at home base, while the other was available for a second start at the remote site, when the aircraft needed to take to the air again. Spare cartridges were also included in the equipment that the ground crews brought to the remote sites.

Winter was still with us and the need for cold weather clothing was an absolute must. However, because the squadron had been formed so late in the year, our stores had been unable to obtain normal RAF issue parka jackets that were typically issued to flight line workers on a loan basis. Nevertheless, our resourceful stores staff was able to obtain a consignment of Arctic jackets as a stopgap measure. The tan coloured jackets kept us warm, but were a little peculiar in appearance. To don one of the jackets, it was necessary to pull it on over the head because it was a one-piece garment without an opening at the front.

***

The hood was cone shaped, not unlike that sported by the little gnome ornaments that some people have in their gardens. Very quickly, they came to be known as "Noddy jackets" after a children's' TV cartoon gnome character of the same name, because of the resemblance of the jacket's hood to his cap.

KESTRELS ARRIVE 23

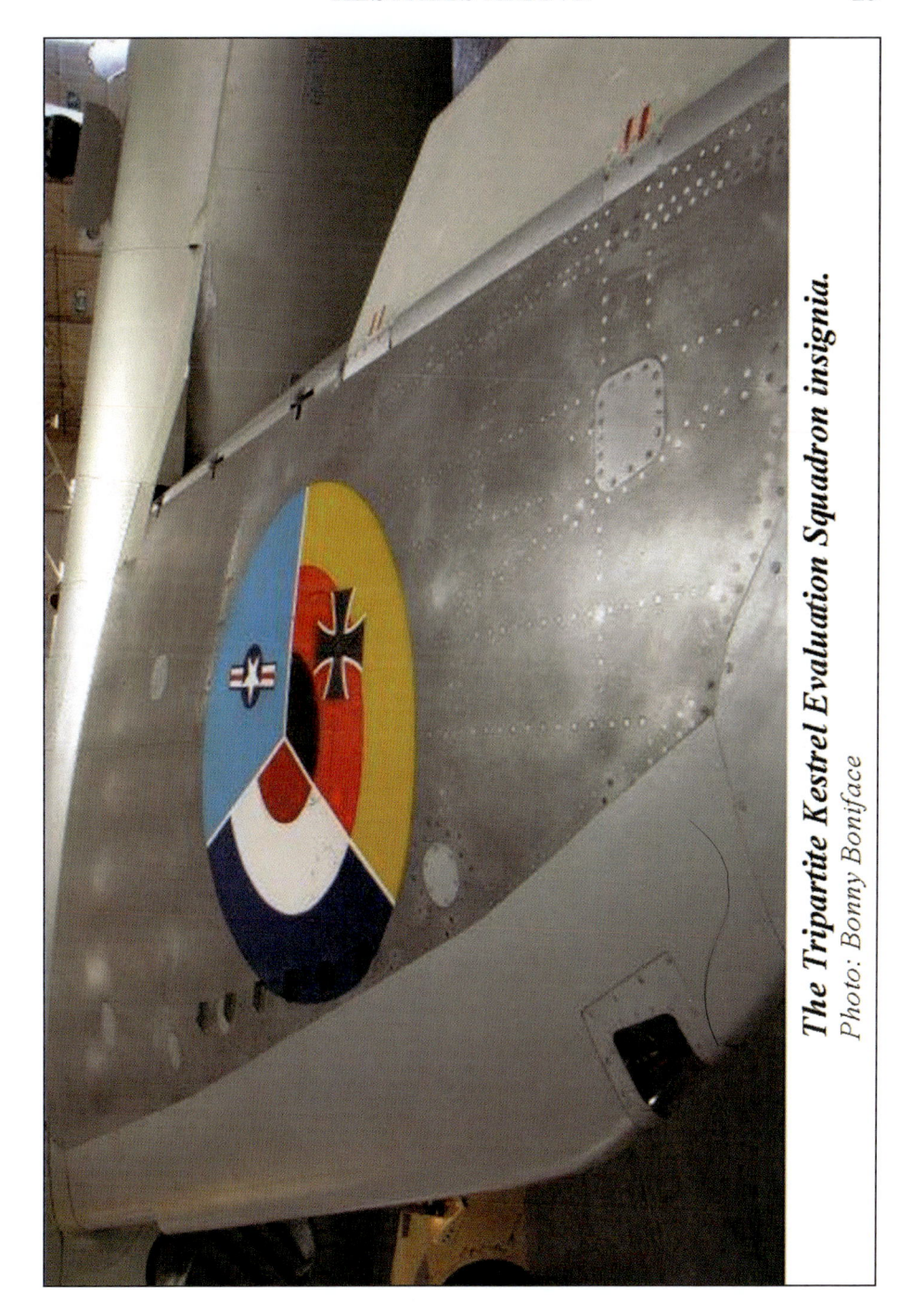

The Tripartite Kestrel Evaluation Squadron insignia.
Photo: Bonny Boniface

Kestrel XS690 on display at its current home, Pima Air Museum, Tucson, Arizona in its original Kestrel Squadron livery, but wearing a non-Kestrel nose cone.
(Photo courtesy of Pima Air Museum)

Engine start!
(Photo by Günter Findiesen)

An early shot of four squadron ground crew members with a Kestrel prior to it having its number applied to the nose. L to R; Cpl. Mike Oliver (RAF), unidentified member, Cpl. Clive Cox (RAF), Spec. 5 Gerald Gipson (US Army).
(Photo courtesy of Bonny Boniface)

Bonny Boniface "modelling" the "Noddy" cold weather jackets the RAF ground crews were issued with during the winter of 1964. It was replaced later with standard RAF cold weather clothing just in time for the following winter.
(Photo courtesy of Bonny Boniface)

Chapter 5: Personal Transportation Ups and Downs

It was around this time that I bought a second-hand car because the motor scooter was not very practical when it came to shopping for groceries in Fakenham, which was the nearest large town a few miles away. On our way there one day, Pam and I noticed a black Austin A30 at a small used car dealership. There was a sign in the car window offering it for £120, which just happened to be the full extent of our meagre savings. Thrilled at the thought of being able to afford our very own first car, we stopped and quickly closed the deal with the sly owner. However, to paraphrase an old saying, Purchase in Haste and Repent at Leisure! Before buying the car, I should have sought the advice of some of my more car-savvy colleagues. Phil May, our other next-door neighbour, owned an older Jaguar on which he was constantly tinkering. He, and others, would probably have advised us to run a mile in the opposite direction from the wily old dealer, but sadly their advice came much too late – a case of being wise after the event.

To begin with, the car had apparently been involved in a crash at some point in its life and the damage, although disguised, left it with an ill-fitting driver's side door. Daylight could clearly be seen through the gap between door and doorframe, but blinded by the euphoria of first-time car ownership, I was too naïve to notice that when first looking the car over. A strenuous test drive by an experienced car owner might also have highlighted some of the other problems that plagued me later on. On the plus side – most of the knowledge I ever gained concerning car maintenance and repair was thanks to that hapless little Austin.

The first major mechanical problem began in small way, when the starter operated. At first, it was a mild thudding noise as the engine turned over, but over the course of a few weeks, the thudding gradually became more pronounced. Then it all came to a head one Saturday when we returned to the car after doing some shopping in Kings Lynn. Instead of the chug-chug-chug that we were by now accustomed to when I pulled on the starter knob, we were startled by a high-pitched whine from the starter motor that became increasingly shriller and louder until I quickly let go of the starter knob. Obviously, the starter motor was not engaging with the engine, but that's as far as my assessment of the problem went. I climbed out of the car, threw up the bonnet to expose the engine and peered in at it, although I had no idea what to look for. Actually, I was more intent on pondering what to do next. Where could I get help? How were we going to get home? Pam wanted answers to these questions, as well as an explanation of the problem – an explanation that I just didn't have. Just then, a knight in shining armour came riding along on his pure white stallion. Well, he wasn't really wearing armour, nor was he riding a horse. In fact, he was just an ordinary bloke in his early to middle forties, but he might as well have been a knight in shining armour as far as I was concerned, because he soon got us out of our dilemma. He had heard the whine of the starter from across the car park and, probably noticing my clueless reaction, had come over to offer some assistance.

"Sounds like you have a spot of bother there mate," he announced, as he approached.

I looked around in surprise and then agreed.

"It sounds like you might be missing some teeth on your ring gear," he offered.

I had no idea what he meant. "What's a ring gear?"

"It's the gear teeth on your flywheel that the starter engages with to turn over the engine," he explained. "Tell you what. Try putting your gear lever in fourth gear and then we'll rock the car backwards and forwards a bit to see if we can get it to stop at a spot that has teeth."

I shifted the gear lever into fourth, as he suggested, then we both pushed the car backwards and forwards a few times.

"Try it now," the man suggested.

This time, when I pulled the starter, there was the familiar chug-chug and then the engine started. I profusely thanked the gentleman for his good advice and help before heading for home.

For a few weeks, rocking the car became a common occurrence, because the flywheel seemed to favour stopping in that worn position. However, I knew the problem needed to be fixed. Having it repaired at a garage was out of the question because we simply couldn't afford it, so I decided to tackle the job myself. Fortunately, the former USAF occupants of the Sculthorpe base had put in an automobile service station near their PX, when the base had been in their hands. Their legacy was a disused building that contained a service pit, which I and other car owners – Americans and British alike – used frequently, although I'm sure I must have held the record for occupying it the most.

After seeking much advice and guidance from anyone and everyone who knew how to do the job, I used the service pit to get at the problem. I also replaced the clutch assembly at the same time because it had been slipping and would probably have been the next thing to fail.

Over time, one of the half-shafts driven by the rear axle broke, and the pit was a real boon for the removing the differential rear axle and extracting the small stub of the broken half-shaft. Later, an exhaust valve burned out, although it wasn't necessary to use the pit on that occasion. However, a window-lit bench in another part of the same building was convenient to grind in a new exhaust valve after having removed the cylinder head.

A nearby car repair garage, quaintly named 'The Four Winds' (we referred to it as the Four Farts), was another blessing, given that we were really out in the middle of nowhere. It sat at the junction of the main Kings Lynn to Fakenham Road and the minor road that led up to the Sculthorpe married quarters. The proprietor was one of the experts that I consulted, and he generously offered valuable advice on how to go about some of the mechanical repairs, even though he could have easily refused on the basis that I was depriving him of business. Maybe the reason for this was that I purchased parts from him, both new and salvaged. The ring gear was one example of a new part which, for a small additional price, he included the removal of the damaged ring gear from the flywheel and the fitting of the new one. I would not have been able to perform this operation by myself because the ring gear was a shrink-fit and needed the application intense heat from an oxy-acetylene torch to expand both the old and new ring gears so that one could be removed and the other fitted.

As for salvaged parts, a large portion of the land on which the garage sat served as a graveyard for several scrapped vehicles that had seen happier days. One of the cars dumped there amongst the overgrown weeds was a scrapped Austin that, by very good fortune, was a 1956 A30 model just like mine. The garage proprietor was only too pleased to sell me parts from the scrapped A30, when they were an acceptable alternative to expensive new parts, although this usually meant having to remove the desired part myself.

It took several months of work, but eventually the car was in reasonably good mechanical condition. That was just as well because Pam had started taking driving lessons with a driving school and passed her driving test at Kings Lynn during the summer of 1965. Later, she got a Christmas seasonal job at Boots the Chemist in Fakenham, (she had been a long-time Boots employee in Lincoln), so needed the use of the car to get there. Meanwhile, through the generosity of my squadron colleagues, I was able to get lifts to and from work each day.

A typical Austin A30 that's in much better condition than my old jalopy.

Chapter 6: Disaster on Day One

By the end of March 1965, two more Kestrels, XS695 and XS696, had been delivered to the squadron, with six more in the pipeline. With these two aircraft, it was possible for continuation training to proceed so that the pilots and ground crews could gain operational experience. Although, with so few aircraft and so many pilots, there was a lack of opportunities for the latter to maintain flying proficiency, so a Hawker Hunter F6 was loaned to the squadron for this purpose. Eventually, three Hunters were on loan to the squadron to be used for pilot proficiency. They were also used as chase planes to follow the Kestrels, especially after any major maintenance on the latter, such as an engine change.

The pilots, in particular, concentrated on building on the experience they had gained at Dunsfold. In the beginning, they took off and landed conventionally, but before long, they were using both the VTOL (Vertical Takeoff and Landing) and the STOL (Short Takeoff and Landing) configurations for both of these activities. Although the VTOL mode was an important element of the trials, using it reduced engine life by a drastic amount and it was therefore employed sparingly. It turned out to be more suited when operating from hard standings such as concrete or asphalt, where the presence of debris could be more easily controlled. On the other hand, when operating in the VTOL mode from unprepared sites, such as grassy areas or bare hard-packed earth, the downwards jet efflux tended to kick a cloud of dust and debris into the air. This interfered with the pilot's line of sight and increased the risk of Foreign Object Damage (FOD) due to debris being ingested into the engine, with the very real risk of catastrophic engine failure as a result. When operating from unprepared sites, they found that the STOL mode worked best because the Kestrel's slow rate of forward travel as it landed or lifted off the ground at a steep angle avoided both visibility and ingestion problems.

Perhaps a comment in the previous paragraph that Kestrel's Pegasus engine life was severely affected when the aircraft operated in VTOL mode warrants a little more explanation. The life of any jet engine is directly related to the temperature at which the hot sections of the engine are permitted to operate. More power requires more fuel and more fuel means higher operating temperature. Temperature has an impact on the metals and metal alloys used in the high temperature sections of the engine, such as combustion chambers and turbine blades. Although high temperature alloys are used in these areas, and creative strategies are employed to keep them as cool as possible, there is an increased rate of turbine blade erosion associated with increases in the engine temperature. This manifests itself as reduced power over time, which translates as reduced engine life. The Kestrel operating in VTOL mode was an extreme example of this because the amount of thrust needed to support the full weight of the aircraft while, at the same time, air was being bled off to the directional control "puffer jets" from the high pressure engine compressor. Both of these conditions demanded much more fuel than was required in forward flight, or even in STOL operation. Obviously, the engine temperature soared in this condition, drastically devouring the Pegasus engine life. In real time, and under certain circumstances, this could be as little as one hour of operation between engine changes. Engines with expired life were returned to Bristol Siddeley for dismantling, inspection and re-blading as necessary.

***

The first official day of the trials was the 1st of April 1965. Unfortunately, it did not go well. The honour of making the first and, as it turned out, the only flight that day was bestowed on US Army pilot Lieutenant Colonel Solt, who was also a Squadron Deputy Commander jointly with Colonel Barkhorn. The plan was for Lt. Col. Solt to perform a short take off from the main West Raynham runway. In anticipation of witnessing the historic event, Wing Commander Scrimgeour, together with a group of high-ranking officers, had gathered near the end of the runway, unaware that the drama about to be enacted before them was going to be far from any of their expectations.

Meanwhile, back on the hard standing in front of the squadron hangar, Lt. Col. Solt strapped into the cockpit of Kestrel XS696 (number 6), with the assistance of a groundcrew member. After handing each of the shoulder straps to the pilot, two for the parachute harness and two for the seat harness, the groundcrew member's final task was to remove the ejection seat safety pin from the upper black and yellow striped activating handle, thus arming the seat. He showed the pin to the Lt. Col. Solt to confirm that the seat was armed and then stowed it in a special holder on the side of the seat. Having performed this important safety function, the groundcrew member descended the cockpit access ladder, moved it from the aircraft and laid it down with the other the ground equipment, at a safe distance from the Kestrel.

Lt. Col. Solt proceeded to carry out his cockpit checks and, once satisfied that all was well, gave the "engine start" hand signal to the ground crew; a twirling motion of the hand with forefinger pointed upwards. The lead groundcrew member was in position facing the pilot, awaiting the signal and, on getting it, looked around the aircraft to make sure all was clear before repeating the same signal back to the pilot. Almost immediately, a dark column of smoke shot up into the air from the top of the aircraft as the starter cartridge exhaust vented to the atmosphere. The engine rapidly spooled up, providing hydraulic pressure to the aircraft systems. The small, black Ram Air Turbine (RAT) that conspicuously popped up out of its housing on top of the fuselage when hydraulic pressure was absent, now retracted and two little doors automatically closed over it to "clean up" the upper fuselage.

RAF Corporal Boniface, standing off to one side, was satisfied to see the RAT disappear into its housing because he had worked on it during his entire lunch period when it had failed to retract on a previous start. He then stayed on to assist as a member of the groundcrew.

Once his post engine-start checks were complete, the pilot gave the "chocks away" signal. The lead groundcrew member signalled to one of the other men to pull the main-wheel chock away. Once all was clear, he used standard NATO marshalling signals to guide the pilot out of the flight line before giving the turn signal that directed him towards the taxiway. The groundcrew then tidied up the flight line area from which the Kestrel had just vacated, while the aircraft taxied out of sight towards the north-eastern end of the runway. So far, all was going as planned.

Wing Commander Scrimgeour and his guests watched as the Kestrel rounded the corner of the taxiway onto the runway threshold and lined up with the centreline before coming to a halt. After a few moments, clearance for takeoff came from the control tower and the pilot opened the throttles to commence his takeoff roll. The Kestrel began to move, but the onlookers immediately perceived that something was wrong. Within the space of a few hundred feet, the aircraft veered dramatically to the left, leaving a long black skid mark on the asphalt, and careened on to the grass at the side of the runway. On contacting the rough ground, the starboard outrigger sheared off, causing the wingtip that it supported to touch the soft, grassy earth. Immediately, the aircraft spun around horizontally in what is often referred to by those in aviation circles as a ground loop, eventually coming to rest facing inwards towards the runway.

Wing Commander Scrimgeour must have been hard pressed to believe his eyes as he witnessed the nightmarish disaster playing out before him. Shaking off any feelings of disbelief, he quickly gathered his wits and sprang into action to be the first to rush over to the doomed Kestrel and help Lt. Col. Solt get safely out of the wrecked cockpit. The Wing Commander later received the Queen's Commendation for Brave Conduct in recognition of his action, the citation reading, "in recognition of his gallantry and determination in rescuing the pilot from a crashed and burning aircraft, on 1st April 1965."

With the incident occurring in full view of the control tower, there was no time lost in dispatching emergency vehicles to the scene. Although the Kestrel did not actually catch fire, contrary to the Wing Commander's citation and many reports on the Internet, the fire crew quickly covered the crashed Kestrel with fire retardant foam as a precaution against this happening. The burst tyres may have started burning, but this small conflagration would have been quickly extinguished by the foam. When the emergency crews arrived on the scene, the pilot was still being extricated from the cockpit so they took over and completed the rescue. He was then quickly transferred to hospital, having suffered some minor injuries that needed medical attention.

DISASTER ON DAY ONE

Meanwhile, back on the flight line, Bonny Boniface and the other ground crew members were puzzled at what they perceived to be a delay in the Kestrel's takeoff, but when they saw the fire engines race off towards the runway, they knew something had gone wrong. Although unable to see what had actually happened, instinct propelled them to jump into their Land Rover and rush to the scene so they could help in any way possible. Shortly afterwards, Bonny took some photos of the crashed Kestrel, which are reproduced below.

The circumstances behind the mishap came to light at the inevitable board of enquiry. The US Army did not, and still does not operate high performance combat jet aircraft. That particular service is more accustomed to using helicopters and fixed wing piston engine aircraft such as the De Havilland Beaver on loan to the squadron. Although the Army pilots assigned to the squadron had undergone conversion training on jets, it was perhaps not enough. For some reason, (possibly associated with pre-takeoff check procedures relating to piston engine aircraft that he was normally accustomed to flying), the Lt. Col. Solt applied the parking brake when he took up position at the end of the runway. Then, prior to commencing his take off run, he forgot to release it, which meant that the main wheels were locked from the moment he started to move down the runway. With the engine operating at a high power setting, both wheels were dragged in a long skid until the port side tire burst. This caused the Kestrel to yaw to the left and off the runway onto the grass, where it dug in and came to rest. This was a rather embarrassing start to the trials, but happily, no life was lost, nor any more aircraft lost, although one did get a little badly bent later on.

Fortunately, the only notable civilian awareness of the incident surfaced as a grainy, distant photograph taken from the narrow east-west country lane near the northern end of the runway. The photo appeared in the local Fakenham newspaper, but never made it into any of the major press.

US Navy Commander Tyson visited Lt. Col. Solt in hospital, but also had the unpleasant task of informing him that his days of flying the Kestrel were over. When discharged from the hospital, Solt was quietly repatriated to the Pentagon in Washington D.C. where he took up a desk job as liaison officer for the Kestrel Squadron. We never saw him again and his place on the squadron was quietly filled by Major P. Curry, US Army, shortly afterwards. Commander Tyson succeeded him as Deputy Squadron Commander.

Because the unfortunate Kestrel sustained so much major damage, it was declared a write-off and the wreckage returned to Hawker Siddeley's Dunsfold factory as salvage. This left the squadron short of one aircraft for the remainder of the evaluation. Nevertheless, the trials proceeded, even though we were now limited to just two Kestrels for most of April. During this time, the aircraft were operating only from the West Raynham airfield and in STOL configuration for the most part. VTOL operation was strictly limited during this phase, typically being employed only when there was some visiting bigwig to impress, of which there were several. Also, we were heavily overmanned to be operating under these conditions, although it was only temporary. Our numbers were better utilized later, when more aircraft arrived from the factory and when we had transitioned to operating the Kestrels from remote locations. This, after all, was one of the major objectives of the trials. As it was, several personnel were assigned to second line servicing in one of the other hangars, and many others, such as Armourers, Safety Equipment technicians and Photographic personnel, were diverted into the appropriate sections on the station that specialized in those trades. Meanwhile, in April, much idle time was spent in crew-rooms or, in my case, also hanging around in the Electrical and Instrument Section.

***

The fact that we had only two aircraft on the entire squadron meant that I had a lot of time on my hands, in between technical tasks. This provided me with an opportunity to make good on a long overdue career improvement. At the time of joining the squadron, I had held the rank of Junior Technician for 4½ years, although it was only necessary to remain in that rank for 3 years before being time qualified for promotion to Corporal. Therefore, I was 18 months overdue to move up that next rung on the career ladder. The stumbling block was of my own making. Besides the 3-year qualifying period as a Junior Technician, promotion to Corporal was awarded only if the Junior

Technician had passed a trade test exam paper consisting of 100 multiple-choice questions. The opportunity to take the exam came around only once a year so the consequence for failing, if the time qualification had been satisfied, was to remain a J/T for at least one more year. I had taken the exam every year since becoming a J/T, but only half-heartedly, and consequently failed to achieve the required pass mark. The open secret to passing the exam was, as I was very well aware, the setting aside of personal time in which to study the RAF Trade Training Manual (Air Publication, or AP as it was more commonly referred to) appropriate to one's trade. However, there had been other priorities in my former life as a single airman – not least the courtship of my then girlfriend Pam, with whom I spent most of my off duty evenings and weekends. Now, newly married to Pam, life and its priorities had changed. Searching questions were asked "in the house" about my stalled promotion, but there was no longer any excuse. The upshot was that Pam strongly encouraged me to study for the test, not least because the extra income would help improve our standard of living.

More encouragement came in the person of Chief Tech. Clive Meeks, who was also an electrical SNCO in the E&I Section. Before joining Kestrel Squadron, Clive had been a member of the RAF Trade Standards & Testing Squadron (TSTS) – the organization that created the multiple-choice questions used in trade-test exam papers. TSTS had a dual role; firstly ensuring the standard of training for RAF tradesmen was maintained at the highest possible quality and the level of knowledge and expertise of tradesmen moving up through the ranks was appropriate to the rank to which they were being promoted, and secondly its involvement in the creation of servicing procedures for all RAF aircraft.

Clive pointed out that, in most cases, the correct answer to each question on the exam paper was lifted verbatim from the Trade Training AP. If a person hadn't studied the AP, he or she wouldn't always be able to select the correct answers and, statistically, would not achieve the necessary 60% needed to pass the exam. This was especially true for questions relating to electrical systems on aircraft with which I was unfamiliar, such as the Canberra and Britannia, because I had never been exposed to them in the normal course of my service. The trade training manual did, however, cherry-pick a variety of systems from different modern aircraft to familiarize trainees with their complexities. Acting on Clive's good advice, I signed out a Trade Training AP from the station library and began to study intensely both at home and at work, when there was no other call on my time. It was also helpful to have Clive there to answer questions, or to quiz me on the contents of the chapters.

When exam time came, I felt more confident than in the past. That confidence was well founded because, when the results came through several weeks later, the news was good. I had passed the exam. However, it took a few more weeks before the promotion appeared on the station Personnel Occurrence Reports (POR's), so I still had some time to soldier on as a lowly J/T.

***

The last two weeks of April 1965 saw the arrival of two more of our Kestrels from Dunsfold, then three more in the first week of May. However, we would not get the last aircraft, XS690 (number 0), until the second week of August because it had suffered heavy landing damage at Dunsfold and needed repair. Nevertheless, with seven aircraft now available, the squadron was able to dramatically ramp up the evaluation trials.

DISASTER ON DAY ONE 43

XS 695 executes a short landing on a rough strip of grass at the Pickenham remote site.
(*Photo courtesy of Günter Findiesen*)

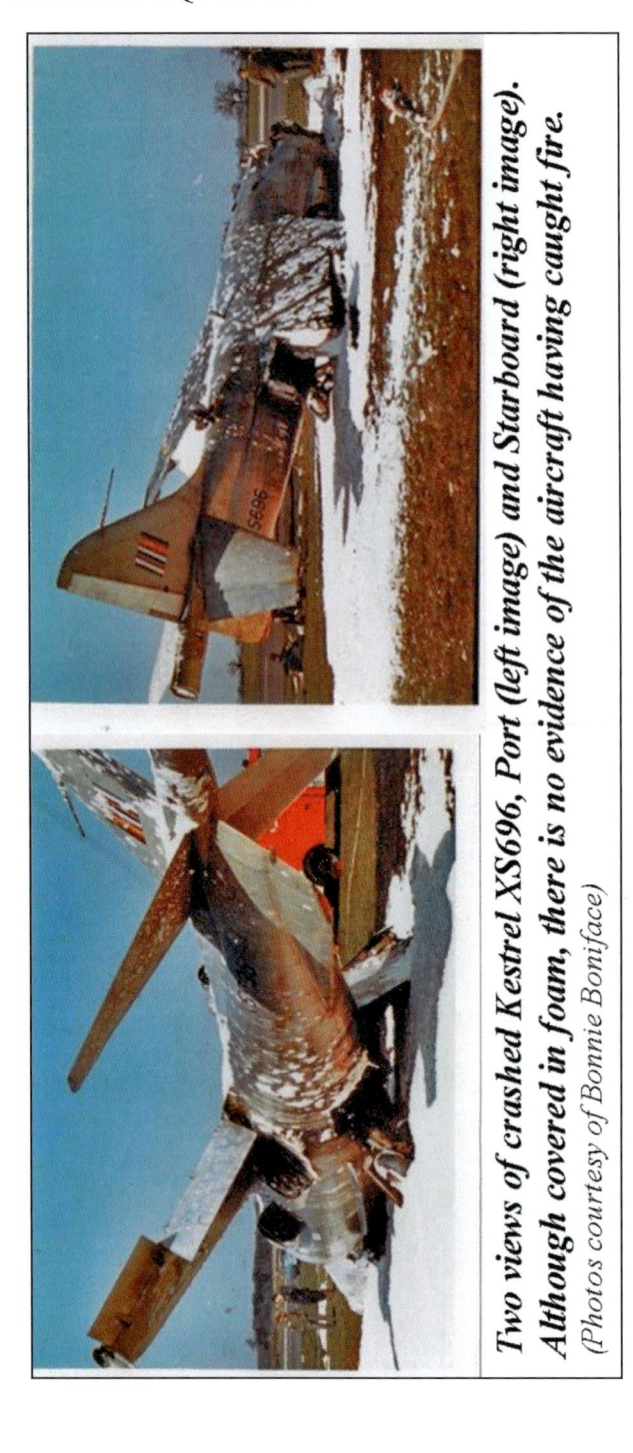

Two views of crashed Kestrel XS696, Port (left image) and Starboard (right image). Although covered in foam, there is no evidence of the aircraft having caught fire. (Photos courtesy of Bonnie Boniface)

DISASTER ON DAY ONE 45

Lineup of seven of our nine Kestrels at RAF West Raynnham.
(Squadron publicity photo)

Chapter 7: *Ubendum and Webendum*

After a few weeks of the trials being confined only to West Raynham airfield, the squadron was ready to operate the Kestrel at remote locations. Typically, a convoy of three-tonner lorries, a bus, Land Rovers and various other vehicles, including a mobile red and white chequered Air Traffic Control "ice cream wagon," would leave West Raynham each morning to head for the location *d'jour*. At first, this was nearby RAF Bircham Newton, where we operated from a large expanse of tall grass far out on the airfield. The first operations at that site began on the 31st of May 1965.

On one such outing to Bircham Newton, the unfortunate American air traffic controller, Sgt. Perry, who was supervising air movements from the "ice cream van" suffered a serious allergy attack caused by pollen blowing off the tall grass that surrounded us on all sides. The poor man's face was red; his eyes had puffed up to the extent that they were nearly closed. Because of this assault on his allergic system, he was barely able to function. Eventually, one of the RAF air traffic controllers arrived at the site to relieve Sgt. Perry of his post, who was then driven back to West Raynham and presumably to some welcome medical aid to provide him with relief from his symptoms.

Later, RAF North Pickenham (a former Thor missile site) was added as a remote location and later still, the Standford Battle Area. At the latter site, during a four-day exercise, the squadron operated in a role designed to evaluate its ground support capabilities. For the purpose of the exercise, local control of the Kestrels was given over to a British Army Air Support Officer. However, the outcome was only successful in demonstrating that the Army needed to be much better acquainted with the Kestrel's capabilities.

Sometimes, special surfaces of various materials were used, such as a sprayed-on polyester resin that hardened into a landing/takeoff surface within an hour of application to an otherwise unprepared surface, or interlocking aluminium planks, or impregnated cloth membranes. Vertical and STOL operations were carried out onto and off these surfaces to determine their usefulness in minimising the soil erosion resulting from jet down-blasts. The erosion problem was of particular interest to Mr. Hindley-Maggs, a Ministry of Defence (MOD) civilian scientist, who regularly accompanied us to the sites.

On 13 October 1965, a privately owned, wooded area known as Raby's Wood, was used for the first time. On landing at this site, the Kestrels taxied into small clearings, where they hid out under the cover of trees. The trees didn't hide everything, however, so we completed the job by covering the aircraft and vehicles with camouflage netting to mimic a real life scenario in which the aircraft were operating from a forward base in a wartime situation. Other Kestrels played the role of aggressors, photographing our general location with their nose cameras during simulated attacks. The photos were later displayed on the squadron notice board, with notations pointing out areas where parts of vehicles or aircraft were visible, indicating that the camouflage netting had not been used to fullest effect. However, with the benefit of experience, we got much better at playing these "hide and seek" games.

It was also on this date that Colonel Barkhorn severely damaged Kestrel XS689, during a rolling vertical landing, by drastically cutting back on engine power while still a few feet off the ground. I did not personally witness this event, but others mentioned that the aircraft was still about three feet off the ground when the Colonel pulled the throttle all the way back. USAF Tech. Sergeant Chuck Massey recalls Barkhorn quipping, "Well, that's another Allied plane I've managed to damage," as Massey helped him out of the cockpit. The resulting heavy landing caused so much damage to the Kestrel's undercarriage that the aircraft had to go back to Hawker Siddeley for repair and was unavailable for the remainder of the trials.

That incident and the earlier loss of XS696 were both due to pilot error, but another incident, which could have resulted in the endangerment to the pilot's life or limbs and loss of the aircraft, turned out to be an issue of MOD policy. In this case, the pilot did the right thing. It happened when RAF Flt. Lt. "Porky" Munro was returning to West Raynham at the end of a sortie. He intended to conclude the flight with a Short Landing on the main runway using vectored thrust, but when attempting to rotate the thrust nozzles from the conventional flight position to that for vectored flight, he felt an unusual restriction in the operation of the nozzle angle control lever. Suspecting this might develop into a more serious problem, Porky decided he needed to get the Kestrel on the ground quickly, and prudently opted for a "conventional" landing. Because of the urgency of the situation, his landing speed was higher than it would have been for a planned conventional landing; consequently, one of the main undercarriage tyres blew out when the wheels touched down on the tarmac. Porky was still able to taxi the Kestrel to the flight line, where he parked the aircraft and shut down the engine. He related his experience to the groundcrew member helping him out of the aircraft and then inspected the damaged undercarriage before walking towards the hangar, feeling a little dejected because of the burst tyre. Partway between the hangar and the flight line, however, the engine fitter carrying out the after flight inspection called for him to return. When Porky got back to the Kestrel, the engine fitter pointed to several nuts that were lying on the bottom of the engine air intake area. Investigation revealed that the nuts, 13 in all, were associated with blade retention on the turbofan assembly and one or more had probably ended up in the nozzle rotation mechanism, causing the interference that Porky experienced. This was obviously a serious problem as it could have led to the loss of the aircraft and possibly serious injury, or worse, to Flt. Lt. Munro.

It would have been difficult to determine if any blades were loose during pre-flight inspections because, by design, the titanium fan blades fitted loosely into their sockets in the hub disc. When an engine "wind-milled" during shutdown, or when a Kestrel was parked facing into the wind, the fan blades could be heard rattling as the fan assembly freewheeled. However, when the engine was operating, the action of air being drawn into the intake forced the fan blades to pivot forward by a small amount. When this happened, "snubbers" near the tip of each blade butted up against those on the neighbouring blades, effectively locking them in place to form a contiguous disc. This is common on modern bypass turbofan engines, of which the Pegasus is but one example.

The above incident can be directly related to the intervals between Pegasus engine overhauls. Because this revolutionary engine was still in development, the initial directive called for all engines to be removed from the Kestrels when no more than 15 hours of engine life had been expended so that the engine manufacturer, Bristol Siddeley, could dismantle them for inspection. A Flight Data Recorder recorded engine-operating temperatures during every sortie. This was because the engine's life accelerated drastically when it operated at higher than normal temperatures, such as when performing purely vertical take-offs or landings. In other words, just a few minutes in "the hover" could equate to a few hours of normal life. The Flight Data Recorder provided a means by which the actual engine life expended during a sortie could be calculated using the recorded information. Therefore, depending on how much vectored thrust (any position of the nozzles other than horizontal for conventional flight) was used, 15 hours of engine life could be used up in as little as a one-hour sortie.

The goal set by the MOD was for the time between overhauls (TBO) to be expanded gradually to 50 hours during the Evaluation, in a series of steps; namely 25 hours, 40 hours and finally the desired upper limit of 50 hours. However, the MOD was also anxious to achieve the 50 hours TBO level as soon as possible, presumably to control development costs. As a result, Bristol Siddeley was under considerable pressure to reach that goal in the shortest possible time.

Because substantial U.S. government funds had been invested in the Pegasus engine research and development, one of the squadron pilots, USAF Major "JK" Campbell, had also been tasked by his government to follow the engine's development from as early as 1962. JK was outspokenly critical of the pressure that was being exerted on Bristol Siddeley to extend the TBO, believing that the engine internals needed to be more closely monitored than the extended intervals would permit. At the time of Flt. Lt. Munro's incident, the TBO interval had already been increased from 25 hours to 40 hours, despite strong objections from Major Campbell since, in his opinion, current research and development tests did not support the extension. However, the MOD ignored his objections and issued the new 40-hour directive. The incident involving Flt. Lt. Munro occurred when his aircraft's engine life had achieved 37 hours since its previous overhaul, lending strength to the Major's position. In the end, the TBO goal of 50 hours was achieved, in spite of JK's efforts to persuade the MOD to slow the process down.

UBENDUM AND WEBENDUM

***

"Ubendum, Wemendum" is a somewhat wry, unofficial motto of ground crews throughout the RAF and many other air forces. It is aimed at aircrew who are sometimes the source of damage to the aircraft they operate, whether in the air or on the ground. In the early days of Kestrel squadron, one of the most frequent "snags" that returning pilots brought back to the flight line was a broken shear pin in one or both of the aircraft's spindly outrigger legs. The pin was designed to break if the outrigger encountered a heavy load, such as an awkward landing, or from taxiing too fast, but replacing it was "a swine" according to the Airframe Fitters into whose bailiwick befell the difficult task of carrying out the replacement. Several groundcrew members were involved in the operation because the aircraft needed to be jacked up to make the repair and this required the services of more than just one man. As an act of contrition, offending pilots usually made amends to the unhappy groundcrew members by donating a few cans of beer for consumption after duty hours. Later on, however, when our pilots became more experienced, the shear pins tended to remain intact and so unfortunately for the Airframe Fitters and their mates, the beer supply dwindled and then eventually dried up entirely.

***

Occasionally, groundcrew members themselves were the source of some the mishaps. Webendum! There's one particular event that comes to mind.

While landing on the grass airfield at Bircham Newton, Kestrel XS694 suffered some damage to its nose-wheel, making it necessary for the wheel to be changed in situ. On the face of it, this situation was ideal for testing the concept of operating a VSTOL aircraft from a forward base, because performing the task involved only the resources available to the forward base personnel. Normally, with a more conventional type of aircraft, this task would have been performed in a hangar or on the hard surface of the flight line.

In order to remove the damaged wheel, a two-man groundcrew team positioned a small hydraulic "bottle" jack under a jacking point on the nose-wheel leg and proceeded to raise the front end of the aircraft. This action caused the Kestrel to pivot around the centrally positioned main undercarriage – the rear of the aircraft lowering as the front end rose. The nose needed to be raised up a considerable distance before the shock absorber reached its full length of travel and the wheel came off the ground with sufficient clearance for its removal and replacement. Things might have gone well if the operation had been performed on a hard surface, but because the hydraulic jack was supported by nothing more than soft earth, an element of instability was introduced into the process. This may or may not have been foreseen but regardless, the operation proceeded anyway.

When the damaged wheel eventually cleared the ground, one of the team, an Airframe Fitter, sat on the ground with his legs stretched out on either side of it so that he could work comfortably at unscrewing the bolts holding the wheel in place. In the meantime, the hydraulic jack had already tilted slightly out of the vertical, but with the removal of the wheel the whole aircraft began lurching to one side, slowly at first, but then at an increasingly faster rate. The other groundcrew team member, who was already acutely aware of the worrisome tilt, now saw a rapidly deteriorating situation in which the seated airman was probably only moments away from suffering serious injury. Moving quickly, he lunged forward and dragged the man clear with only breathtaking seconds to spare before the jack finally toppled over, sending the nose-wheel leg plunging into the ground, where it buried itself several inches into the soft earth.

The Airframe Fitter was fortunate that his colleague was quick to act; otherwise, he would probably have suffered severe leg injuries. However, the groundcrew were in a much worse predicament. How could they now replace the wheel? To add to their discomfort, they had the anxious pilot on their hands, who was probably wondering how this drama was going to play out. Both men hung their full weight on the rear end of the Kestrel in an attempt to counter-balance the weight of the front end, but this was futile. In the end, help arrived in the form of a Coles crane, which lifted the nose of the Kestrel safely off the ground so that the replacement wheel could be installed.

***

Component failures, (or "snags" in RAF vernacular), could sometimes be more of a problem to cure on the Kestrels than they would on other aircraft, because the Kestrels were really prototypes. There was one such incident in which I was personally involved. A fuel pressure indicator in the cockpit appeared to fail. The indicator was a "doll's-eye" type that was common to many RAF aircraft. When the fuel boost pump was turned off, the doll's-eye showed white, but when the pump was operating, the doll's-eye rotated to display all black. On rare occasions, a doll's-eye would rotate only halfway when the fuel pump turned on, resulting in a part-white, part-black indication, leading to some doubt as to whether the pump was running or not. This was one of those rare occasions.

It was a known fault and the knee-jerk remedy was to replace the doll's-eye because, on face value, it appeared to be faulty, but previous experience with the Vulcan had taught me that this was really not the case. In fact, the cause of the fault was a high resistance that had developed across the fuel pressure-switch contacts that normally closed to energize the doll's-eye. The high resistance was probably due to sparking, or arcing, across the contacts when they opened. The pressure switch was a sealed unit so the only possible cure for the doll's-eye snag was to replace the pressure switch, a job I had done several times in the past. On the Kestrel, however, it was easier said than done, as I was soon to discover.

I made an entry in the aircraft servicing log (Form 700), noting the fault, and then reported it to SCPO Roby. At the same time, mentioning my past experience with this type of indicator. Nevertheless, Roby firmly ordered me to replace the doll's-eye, in spite of my protests. In retrospect, had I been in his shoes, I would probably have given the same order. After replacing the doll's-eye with a brand new one, in itself no easy task in the cramped Kestrel cockpit, the half-white, half-black symptom persisted. When I reported this back to Roby, he then agreed that the pressure switch needed to be replaced.

According to the Kestrel technical documentation, the pressure switch was located behind the cockpit's starboard bulkhead instrument panel, (see page 54). Unfortunately, it was not accessible because the instrument panel was built into the bulkhead and therefore not removable. On normal production aircraft, there would have been an access panel on the outside skin that would have provided a means of accessing the pressure switch, but the Kestrels were been built in such a way that no thought had been given to such conveniences. In the end, and after much persuasion, including consultation with the on-site Hawker Siddeley representatives and the factory, we convinced hangar "boss" M/Sgt. Jones and the Airframe Fitters that we needed to have an access hole cut in the fuselage exterior adjacent to the location of the pressure switch. This was done, accompanied by much grumbling and grousing. When the Airframe Fitters finished their work, I promptly replaced the unserviceable pressure switch and then, when we turned the fuel pump on as a functional check, the doll's eye flicked fully to black, proving that my initial diagnosis had been correct.

***

Aircraft servicing, like any skilled occupation, demands a high degree of concentration on the part of those performing the work. Aircraft technicians are also always keenly aware that the lives of others rests in their hands, so they try to maintain their focus on the task in hand without allowing outside distractions to intrude. Unfortunately, our squadron organization incorporated a particular form of officially sanctioned distraction, namely "Time and Motion" recording, which was as irritating as it was distracting. Most of the young airmen clerks employed as Recorders attempted, with some success, to be both diplomatic and non-intrusive, but apparently, one particular individual never got the message informing him to abide by these desirable virtues.

The Recorders' job was to record the nature of the various tasks involved in evaluating the Kestrel and the amount of time that it took to perform them. This involved not only aircraft flight operations, but also tasks associated with routine maintenance and fault rectification. In the case of aircraft maintenance, most of the Recorders managed to interact with us in a way that was barely noticeable, allowing us to devote our full concentration to the job we were working on. However, there was one exception. He was the Recorder assigned to first-line servicing tasks who sadly lacked the interpersonal skills of his fellow Recorders. Armed with clipboard and stopwatch, his typical approach was to accost a technician involved in a servicing task and bluntly ask, "What are you doing?" Quite often, and depending on the frustration level of the job and the tradesman's temperament, the response could be rather unkind and might even have involved language unfit for delicate ears. Unfazed by this, the Recorder would persist in his enquiry until he got an answer. Then, like a child who continually responds to every answer with the same one-word question, he would follow up with "Why?" It reached the point where, before approaching an aircraft to perform a task, we technicians scanned the hangar, hoping we could get there unnoticed. It rarely worked. The Recorder seemed to possess an uncanny ability that gave him an awareness of our intent, because his bespectacled face soon appeared in the hatchway, or over the side of the cockpit, or wherever we happened to be working, and always followed by his signature question, "What are you doing?" There was no escape!

***

The Kestrel was equipped with another type of recorder, although this particular one was not a person. It was the Flight Data Recorder mentioned earlier – one of those orange coloured so-called "black boxes" that are always sought when civilian passenger aircraft meet with a sad end. The Flight Data Recorder had to be installed before each flight and removed when the aircraft returned. Its purpose was to keep track of the engine exhaust temperature throughout the flight; information needed by the "boffins" to allow them to calculate how much engine life had been used up during the sortie, as explained earlier.

The responsibility for installing and removing the Flight Data Recorder was entrusted to the Instrument technicians. They were also responsible for making sure that the recorded material was passed safely to the boffins to enable them to make their calculations. Installation of the recorder in the aircraft during the pre-flight inspection was a little out of the ordinary, however, because it involved a peculiar secondary task. Not only did the technician install the Flight Data Recorder, but he also installed a common thermos flask – the kind in which to keep liquids hot or cold that an average person could purchase. The flask, in this case, held crushed ice into which a long, thin thermocouple was inserted. The thermocouple was used to provide the "reference" temperature of melting ice (0° Celsius/32° Fahrenheit) for comparison with the engine exhaust temperature thermocouples. The flask of ice was a very simple but effective way of achieving that requirement. A special retaining bracket held the flask in place in the electrical equipment bay, in close proximity to the Flight Data Recorder. Although the flask was removable, its screw-top cap stayed with the aircraft, because it incorporated the reference thermocouple, the other end of which was wired into the aircraft jet pipe temperature measuring circuit. It was the Instrument technicians' responsibility to fill the flask with crushed ice prior to installing it and then to empty it at the end of the sortie, when he removed the Flight Data Recorder.

Rolls Royce Pegasus engine.
Note the "snubbers" on the fan blades.
(Photo by Nimbus227.)

Hovering over a aluminium metal pad, preparing for a vertical landing.
(Photo courtesy of Günter Findiesen)

Kestrel XS 694 descending vertically to land on an aluminium metal pad.
(Photo by Günter Findiesen)

*Kestrel XS 694 after safely performing a vertical landing on an aluminium metal pad.
(Photo by Günter Findiesen)*

Refueling under the trees at the Thetford battle area.
(Photo courtesy of Günter Findiesen)

62 KESTREL SQUADRON

*Operating from the Pickenham remote site.
Note the "convoy" vehicles in the background at right.
(Photo courtesy of Günter Findiesen)*

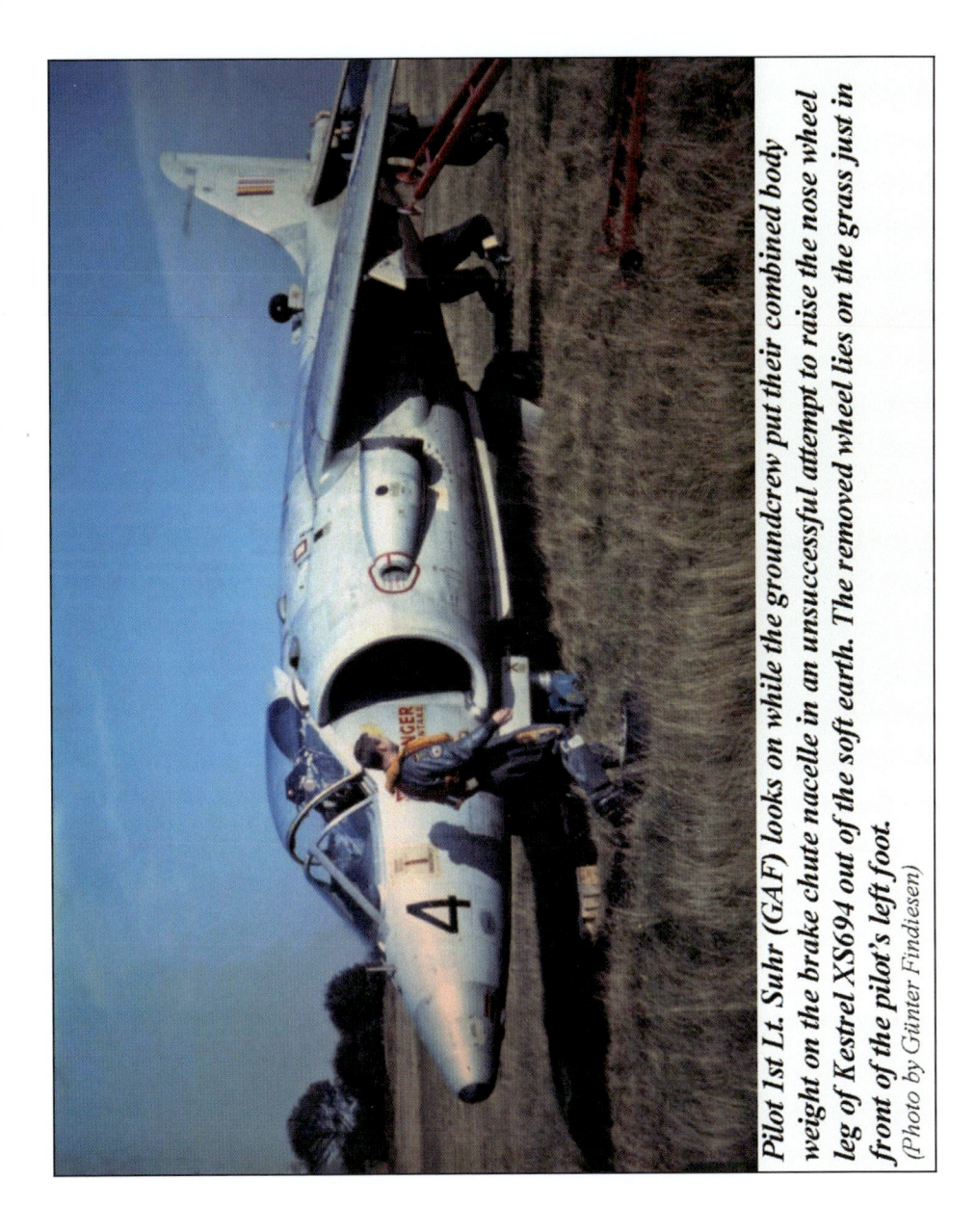

Pilot 1st Lt. Suhr (GAF) looks on while the groundcrew put their combined body weight on the brake chute nacelle in an unsuccessful attempt to raise the nose wheel leg of Kestrel XS694 out of the soft earth. The removed wheel lies on the grass just in front of the pilot's left foot.
(Photo by Günter Findiesen)

The Coles crane rigged to raise the nose of Kestrel XS694. The US Army "Huey" on loan to the squadron can be seen taking off in the background.
(Photo by Günter Findiesen)

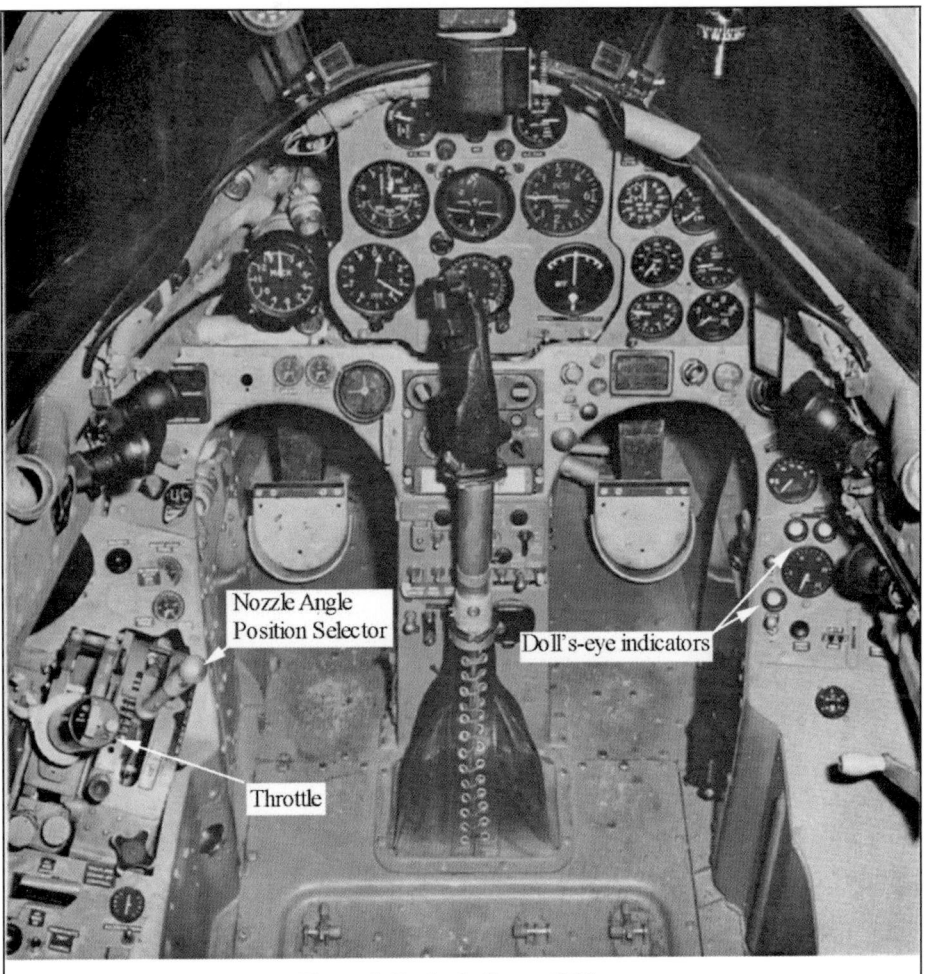

Kestrel Cockpit Overall View
(Photo: Kestrel Evaluation Trials General Report, Supplement A)

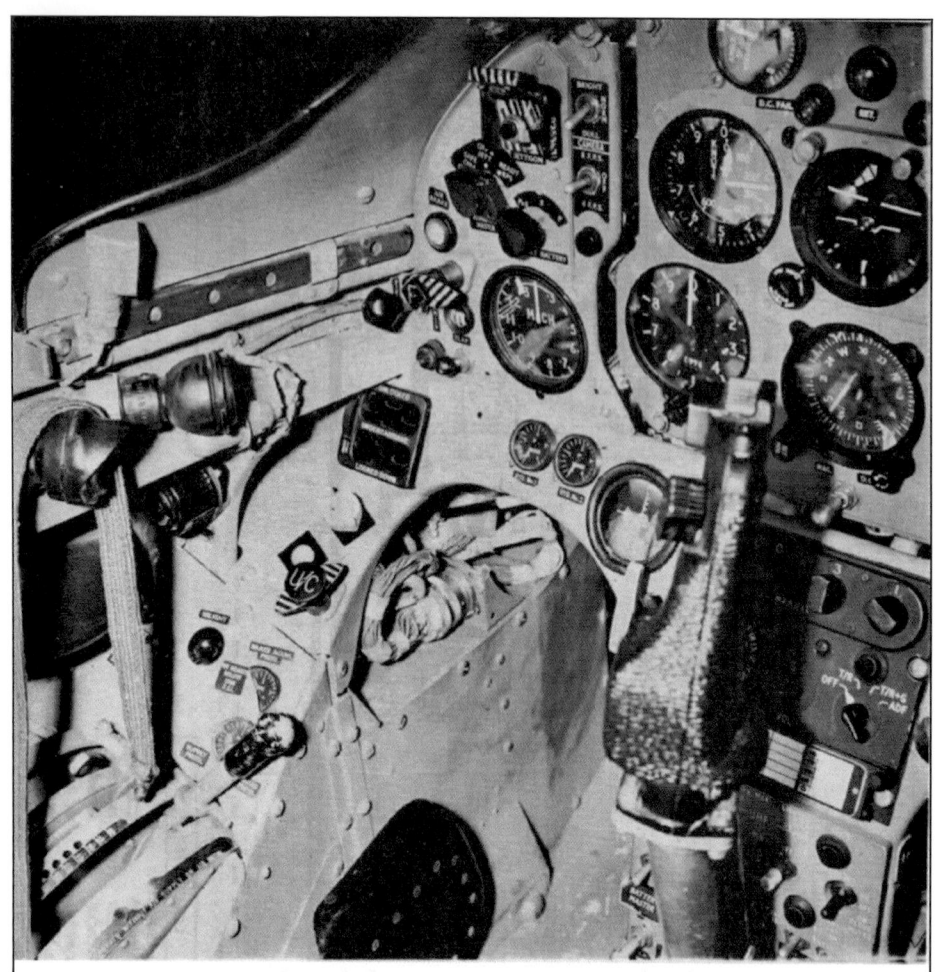

Kestrel Cockpit; Instrument Panel, left side.
(Photo: Kestrel Evaluation Trials General Report, Supplemant A)

Kestrel Cockpit, Main and Lower Instrument Panels.
(Photo: Kestrel Evaluation Trials General Report, Supplemant A)

Kestrel Cockpit; Instrument Panel, right side
(Photo: Kestrel Evaluation Trials General Report, Supplemant A)

Chapter 8: *Working with the Americans*

Back then, in the mid-1960s, Americans drove cars that were much larger, more powerful and roomier than British cars of that era. The American automobiles featured huge, flat expanses of bodywork and monster engines that gulped fuel at an amazing rate. Most Americans on the squadron owned brand new cars that they had purchased just prior to their posting to Britain. That was mainly because of a US tax benefit and free shipment of the cars to the UK, both of which made their purchases worthwhile. US Army M/Sgt. Jones drove an enormous, cream-coloured Ford and occasionally gave me a lift into work when my own puny little Austin A30 was laid up due to its latest major malfunction, or Pam needed it to get to her job in Fakenham. The upholstery in the Master Sergeant's car was wine-red faux leather, as was the fascia and door panels. Recessed into the middle of the fascia was small brass plate, probably about 3 inches long and 2 inches high, on which was engraved "Kenneth R. Jones." I remarked on this little touch of egocentricity and was informed that the car dealer had provided it as a gift.

One of the other Americans, a member of the USAF, owned a sportier car. A quiet but friendly chap, "Stew" often came to the disused service station when I was there to change out his rear axle crown and pinion assembly for one with a different ratio. At other times, he would come to change it back to the prior configuration, explaining that one ratio gave him more speed, while the other gave him more power. Nice if you can have it, but my car had a serious deficit with both of those parameters, which no amount of tampering with the rear axle configuration could ever help.

As we became more accustomed to working from remote sites and familiar with their whereabouts, many of us adopted the habit of setting off directly from home in our own cars and drive to the site that would be used for that day's operations, if it were not too far away. On one of these occasions, I got the opportunity to drive one of the big American cars, which was something that I had been dying to do. On this particular morning, I had driven my Austin A30 to the nearby Bircham Newton site where, during the course of the day one of my electrical fitter co-workers, USAF Staff Sergeant Art Snyder, arrived from West Raynham by RAF Land Rover. For some reason, it was necessary for me to go back to the E&I Section at West Raynham, and he was to take over for me at the site. This switchover resulted in both of our cars being where we were not. At first, Art suggested swapping keys, the idea being that I would drive his car from West Raynham to his Sculthorpe residence at the end of the day, while he would bring mine from Bircham Newton. Then he seemed to have second thoughts about it, thinking that I might not be able to handle his car because the controls were on the left-hand side and it had an automatic transmission. However, having had the opportunity temptingly dangled in front of me, I was eager not to let it go, so managed to persuade him that all would be well. And it was. Driving Art's pale blue Ford Galaxie the 8 miles from West Raynham to Sculthorpe was a priceless experience. From behind the steering wheel, the bonnet (or hood as it was called on such cars) stretched out as a vast expanse before me that seemed to turn through the bends and corners before I did. Driving along the twisting Kings Lynn to Fakenham Road was like floating on a cushion of air instead of the sensation of feeling every rut and pebble on the road that my Austin A30 afforded me. Sadly, the experience ended all too soon, when I delivered the Galaxie safely and in one piece to Art's doorstep. He did likewise with my A30, although I wondered how he enjoyed, or more likely disliked, driving an underpowered, draughty, rattling little British car with a manual gear change. He was too polite to say anything negative, but I'm sure he also had an interesting driving experience that day too.

This seems like a good place to comment on what it was like to work so closely and be on the same squadron with members of two other nations' forces, especially the Americans, but I do so with some irony. As with the entirety of this narrative, I have had to mentally return to that time and place, when I was a 24-year-old RAF serviceman, to recall the impressions I had then of my fellow squadron members who not only wore different uniforms but also hailed from different cultures. I should emphasise that from an early age I have always been pro-American. After all, hadn't both nations been on the same side in two wars and didn't we speak the same language? Nevertheless, I soon found out that there was plenty of truth in the

WORKING WITH THE AMERICANS

often-quoted adage, "two peoples separated by a common language," as it relates to the British and the Americans. We were most definitely different. The irony is that several years later, in 1979 to be precise, Pam and I, with our two young daughters, crossed the Atlantic to settle in the New World, eventually becoming United States citizens. So, relating my earlier impressions of the Americans from my Kestrel Squadron days feels almost like a betrayal of my adopted country. In the interests of honesty, however, I need to tell it as I saw it then.

Individually, the Americans were easy to get along with, and generous to a fault. Shortly after acquiring my Austin A30, I was so taken up with the thrill of driving to work in my very own car that I neglected to pay attention to the fuel gauge. The result was that I ran out of petrol on the winding country lane that connected RAF West Raynham to the main Kings Lynn to Fakenham Road and came to an involuntary halt. A few minutes later, an American car came along and, seeing that I had stopped in the middle of nowhere, pulled up behind me. There were two Americans on board, although I only remember that one of them was USAF Staff Sgt. Harvey West, who hailed from the "Deep South" state of Georgia. On learning of my dilemma, he produced a length of rubber tubing from the boot of his car and laughingly informed me, in his Georgian accent, that where he came from they called it a Mississippi gas ticket. He then siphoned a few pints of petrol out of his fuel tank and into a container, which he then transferred into mine, and I was soon on my way again. This type of kindness was typical on an individual basis, but in the overall "tribal" situations, the edges did not always slide smoothly together and could occasionally result in ruffled feathers on one side or the other. The Germans, being small in number, wisely stayed on the sidelines and didn't get involved, nor did they overtly take sides.

At first, there was a kind of "getting to know you" phase, during which everyone put his best face forward. It wasn't too long, however, before a friendly rivalry developed between the RAF and our American fellow squadron-mates, although there were times when the "friendliness" could become a little strained. I don't know if this rivalry extended to the officers, but was certainly very evident amongst the non-officer members of the squadron. Perhaps it shouldn't be a surprise, considering the rivalries that have always existed between different RAF squadrons, or between branches of the British armed services. It was also noticeable that similar rivalries existed between the three US services represented on the squadron. SCPO Roby of the US Navy often used his rank to disparage some of the lower ranking US Army and Air Force members in the E&I Section, but in general, the main rivalry was between the RAF and the Americans. In a nutshell, we RAF lads felt we were the best-trained aircraft technicians in the entire world, whilst our American fellow squadron members believed the same of themselves. In reality, we were all professionals, each being able to rightfully claim the title of "best-trained." However, a particular incident favourably changed my perception of our American colleagues, which I will relate a little later.

Although we shared a common language, which for the most part made communication easy, there are some differences between British and American English that provided fertile ground for miscommunication. Once, while I was towing some ground equipment into the hangar behind a squadron Land Rover, US Army M/Sgt. Jones bellowed a string of words at me from several feet away. It began with "Carlin," which I understood, but the rest of his sentence blurred into something that was completely unintelligible to my ears. He might just as well have been speaking Greek, Outer Mongolian, or Double Dutch for as much sense as I got out of it.

"Pardon?" I politely asked.

This time, I listened carefully and heard him when he repeated, "Carlin, go git that jeep gassed up!" It was the last day of the month, which was when the station Motor Transport (MT) Section routinely wanted all RAF vehicles topped off with fuel so they could keep track of mileage performance. However, the Master Sergeant's order wasn't English as spoken by us natives, although I did realize what he was ordering me to do.

"Oh, you want me to go and get the Land Rover filled up with petrol?" A little sarcastic, but with the thought that we need to teach these colonials how to speak the Queen's English. Jones didn't reply, but he treated me to an angry glare, which was answer enough.

WORKING WITH THE AMERICANS

Our officers sometimes had trouble with the language differences too. There was one story that made the rounds of the squadron. It concerned one of the American pilots, USAF Major Campbell ("JK") who, when not flying, usually walked around with a cigar clenched between his teeth. It seems that on a simulated attack sortie, the designated target was a railway marshalling yard, where the object was to "destroy" the rolling stock, using the Kestrel's nose camera to simulate the aircraft's weaponry. JK returned without having recorded any footage on his camera. During his post-sortie debriefing, the Major complained that he hadn't seen "*any* goddamned stock in the target area." This initially puzzled the RAF debriefing officer, but after some gentle interrogation, he realized that JK had assumed that "stock" referred to cattle, as would be found in an American stockyard.

It wasn't just a question of language; there were also procedural differences. The Americans probably had a more difficult time with this than the RAF because the squadron was organized on the RAF model, which meant that procedures we took for granted were literally and metaphorically foreign to the Americans. For example, our Aircraft Servicing Record (RAF Form 700) was something they had to learn to use, instead of their own documentation. The RAF also observed a strict demarcation between trades, as did the Germans. The Americans, on the other hand, were prone to cross trade boundaries, which sometimes confounded us. Another small cultural difference was that, on a one-on-one level, the Americans addressed their peers, Americans or otherwise, by surname only, whereas RAF airmen addressed colleagues on a first name or nickname basis. To us, using only a surname was impersonal and usually only used by superiors when addressing someone of lesser rank. It was even considered mildly insulting if used by someone of equal status.

The incident that altered my perception of the Americans, hinted at earlier, happened when we were about halfway through the evaluation. Not only did it result in my American fellow squadron members earning my deeper respect, it also provided me with a small glimpse of the stuff from which our German war ace, Colonel Barkhorn, was made.

It began when the pilot of a Kestrel reported an "Engine Fire Warning System" malfunction when he landed his aircraft at the Bircham Newton remote site. Since the fire detection/suppression system was the responsibility of our Electrical trade, Art Snyder and I were able to diagnose that the problem was due to a faulty fire detector, one of several arrayed around the interior of the engine compartment. Unfortunately, the failed detector was located on an area of the engine bay bulkhead that was inaccessible because of the small amount of clearance between it and the engine. With the limited resources available to us out in the field, the best we could do was to wire the faulty detector out of the detection circuit. Doing this fooled the fire warning system into "seeing" that all was well and made the Kestrel flyable for the short hop back to West Raynham. The only other alternative would have been to dismantle the Kestrel and take it back by road on the "Queen Mary" aircraft transporter that was part of our convoy. Problem solved, or so we thought. What we hadn't counted on, however, was that none of the British or American pilots would fly the Kestrel with a partially disabled fire detection system, even though the flight from Bircham Newton to West Raynham would take only a few minutes. However, one of our German pilots did volunteer – the intrepid Colonel Barkhorn. He climbed into the cockpit without the slightest hesitation, strapped in and took off. We supposed that after dodging enemy fighters on the Russian Front, he must have thought that a short hop with a suspect fire detection system was not such a huge risk. And so, the Colonel flew the Kestrel back to West Raynham without incident, although that's not the end of the story.

Next day in the hangar, we electricians were again faced with the task of replacing the faulty fire detector. Because of its inaccessibility, the servicing manual called for the engine to be removed so that we could get to it. We made this requirement known to M/Sgt. Jones and waited in the E&I Section for word that the engine removal had been carried out. This was the RAF way – we worked within the guidelines of the servicing manual specific to our trades. If the manual stated that an engine needed to be removed before we could proceed with a certain task, then that's what the engine people had to do. As it happened, the engine fitters assigned to the removal were all Americans, and they understandably took a dim view of having to pull out the engine – a lengthy, complex operation – for the sake of replacing a paltry little component. Something that in their minds was akin to using a sledgehammer to crack a nut. Soon after we had made our engine removal requirement known, a disgruntled American "Propulsion Specialist" came storming into the E&I Section, demanding to know why the removal was necessary. He argued that there surely must be some way to avoid such a laborious, time-consuming job. Chief Tech. Jim Brookes was not swayed. He had personally checked the location of the detector and ascertained that it was out of the line of sight, although it could be reached blindly by hand. The only way it could be seen, which was essential in order to make the correct electrical connections, was indirectly, by using a mirror and light. Confident in his position, Brookes opened the servicing manual to the specific page and pointed to the paragraph detailing the correct procedure – step 1: remove the engine.

"Okay," the Propulsion Technician retorted, and then announced that he and his crew would change the "godammed" detector themselves. We smugly wished him good luck as he left the room, slamming the door behind him.

For the next couple of hours, we could see the Americans taking turns in contorting themselves to get at the detector. Not only Engine people, but Airframe technicians as well. We wondered how long it would be before they gave up and conceded that removal of the engine was the only way. In the end, however, the laugh was on us because they actually succeeded in removing the bad detector and replacing it with a serviceable one. We inspected the replacement with a "shufty-scope" (a mirror and light bulb on the end of a long, flexible probe) and performed the necessary functional checks. We were humbled – everything was working as it was supposed to. From that time on, I acquired great respect for the Americans' can-do attitude.

Paradoxically, although the Americans seemed to have little hesitation in blurring the lines of demarcation between trades, some American military aircraft maintenance technicians are more specialized than their RAF counterparts. Typically, USAF Aircraft Maintenance Technicians perform normal routine maintenance, but let's say a problem with the hydraulic system comes to light during a pre-flight inspection, an Aircraft Hydraulic Systems *Specialist* would be called in to fix it. Similarly, if a fracture were discovered in the aircraft skin, the Maintenance technician would request the services of an Aircraft Structural Maintenance *Specialist*. Within the RAF trade hierarchy, both of these problems would be the responsibility of an Airframes Fitter. The difference between the Americans' specialization approach and the RAF's all-encompassing approach can be exemplified by another experience, as related to me by "Bonny" Boniface.

While Bonny, a RAF Airframe Fitter, was carrying out a post-flight inspection on Kestrel XS694, shortly after it was delivered from Dunsfold, he noticed there was a 4-inch-long crack in the aircraft skin, around the region of the port intake. As required, he logged the "snag" in the Form 700 (the aircraft's maintenance record) as an "open" entry, meaning that the crack would need to be repaired before the snag entered in the Form 700 could be signed off as complete. He then consulted with Alf Black, the resident Hawker Siddeley representative, about the crack. They both agreed that it should be prevented from propagating further by drilling a small "stop hole" at each end, (in accordance with standard a RAF procedure), and then applying a 6-inch by 6-inch metal patch over the affected area to bring the Kestrel back to full serviceability. This work was not practical while the aircraft was on the flight line, so it was towed into the hangar. Once the aircraft had been properly parked in the hangar, Bonny proceeded to blank off the Port air intake with paper and masking tape before beginning to drill the "stop" holes, using a compressed air driven drill – a "windy drill" in RAF slang.

He was only a few minutes into the operation when M/Sgt. Jones suddenly came rushing up to him in a highly agitated state, crying out as he approached, "Bonny, what in the hell are you doing?"

On being informed that Bonny was proceeding with the repair, Jones reacted with surprise and alarm; he claimed that such an undertaking was a task for specialists, and added that he had already sent for a repair team to come from the USAF Lakenheath base. Bonny calmly assured him that there was no need for the specialists to travel all that way because such metalwork repairs were part of his RAF trade. Jones was unable to accept this explanation, stating that Bonny was only a "systems man," seemingly making that assumption because they had both attended the same Kestrel Hydraulic Systems training course as Bonny. Alf Black and Chief Tech. John Riley, also an Airframe Fitter, joined the discussion; both strenuously assuring Jones that Bonny was fully qualified and highly proficient to perform the repair. Reluctantly, the Master Sergeant accepted their assurances, although he was not at all happy. No doubt, he was thinking of ways to cancel the Lakenheath team without ending up with egg on his face.

When the repair had been completed successfully and professionally, M/Sgt. Jones accepted that our RAF Airframe Fitters were competent to carry out such repairs and other tasks that involved drilling holes in the aircraft skin. However, one task later on nearly defeated them. When flying operations had been going on for a few weeks, it became noticeable that the aircraft skin was being subjected to serious overheating immediately aft of the rear, hot exhaust nozzles, causing it to buckle and wrinkle. This only occurred when the nozzles were in the zero-degree position for conventional flight. Obviously, the problem needed to be corrected before the affected skin failed. Hawker Siddeley's engineers developed a modification for implementation at the squadron level. The modification involved installing titanium heat shields on the aircraft fuselage, immediately downstream of the rear nozzles. The heat shields would be mounted on "stand-offs" that would not only act to insulate affected aircraft skin from the exhaust heat, but would also slightly deflect the hot jet exhaust efflux off to the side by one or two degrees, so that it would be less likely to come into contact with the fuselage. The titanium heat shields duly arrived from the Hawker Siddeley factory and the task of installing them was assigned to the squadron Airframe Fitters. The job seemed simple enough; drill holes in the heat shields and drill matching holes in the aircraft ribs through which attaching bolts would fasten the heat shields to the airframe. The fitters got to work on the modification, but very quickly discovered that normal drill bits wouldn't make the slightest dent in the ultra-hard titanium metal. Not all was lost, however; Hawker Siddeley soon dispatched special diamond-tipped drill bits that were able to cut through the titanium, and so the Airframe Fitters were able to complete the work.

As time passed, and despite being members of three separate nations, we all began to respect each other's skills and strengths, so it's fair to say that by the end of the first year, we managed to come together as a cohesive unit. We RAF men admired and even envied the ways that the Americans had of getting things done. On one occasion, for example, the U.S. Army's De Havilland Beaver developed a serious engine problem that their technicians were unable to rectify on the squadron. Shortly after the army guys requested a replacement engine, a "Huey" (Iroquois UH-1) helicopter flew in from an Army base on the Continent, bringing the replacement engine, which they delivered directly to our hangar. Had the same problem occurred with an RAF aircraft, one can only imagine the red tape and other hurdles we would have encountered to achieve the same result – and the replacement certainly would not have been delivered right to our door by a helicopter.

***

Although it can be said that there was a coming together in the workplace, social life between the British and Americans never really took off. Each side kept mostly to its own. It was as though Lancaster Road (the street dividing the RAF married quarters from the Americans' tobacco houses) was a deep, vast ocean that was rarely crossed on a social basis. I can't say for sure which side was to blame for this, but perhaps there was blame on both sides. It may have partly been due to British insularity, but also maybe partly a "them and us" attitude adopted by the Americans. Much of their social activities were focused around the Lakenheath USAF base, about forty miles distant – a mere trip "down the road" for Americans accustomed to driving long distances. They went there at weekends to shop for groceries at the Base Exchange, where they could buy American brands of foods, household items and other familiar things. In addition, the American children were ferried by bus to Lakenheath each day where they attended the Base's American schools. This was a necessity because of the vast differences in curricula between the British and American educational systems. The Lakenheath Base was also where the Americans filled up their cars with "gas," which was not as heavily taxed as the petrol dispensed at British service stations. The price they paid was reportedly 21 US cents per gallon, equivalent to 1/6d (one shilling and sixpence) in British pre-decimal currency (15p in decimal currency). In contrast, British motorists paid 5/- (five shillings) a gallon, or 25p in British decimal currency. Albeit, because a US gallon is approximately 4/5ths of an Imperial gallon, the Americans actually paid 1/10-1/2 d (one shilling and tenpence-halfpenny) for the equivalent volume, but it was still a great bargain, nevertheless. I believe they also filled jerry cans with petrol and brought them back so they had enough to last until their next trip. Significantly, we never saw any of them patronize the local pubs, or local shop in Fakenham so, in many ways, the Americans were highly insulated from normal British life.

The cultural divide sometimes manifested itself in rather surprising ways. One July Sunday in 1965, Pam and I were enjoying a normal weekend at home, when a sudden loud commotion in the street brought us to our feet and then to the front door to see what was going on. We then watched in awe as a parade of cars travelled slowly along Lancaster Road. High-spirited, cheering Americans leaned out of car windows while honking their car horns and waving Stars and Stripes flags. One individual was actually perched on the roof of a car as it trundled slowly along the street. At first, we didn't understand what the celebration was all about, but then it dawned on us that the date was July 4th - the American Independence Day holiday. Our American neighbours may have been thinking that there could be no better place to celebrate the occasion than right smack dab in the middle of the country from whom their forefathers had won independence.

Although America was the first colony to have gained independence from Britain, it was by no means the only one and it was all just ancient history to us Brits. Many other former colonies and protectorates followed in America's footsteps, achieving their independence right up to the current era, so to the British, 4th of July was just another day, and did not hold the same significance as it did for our transatlantic allies. We watched the parade, occasionally waving pleasantly to the participants, until it had passed. At the same time, we observed that some celebrants were lubricating their exuberance from a plentiful supply of canned adult beverages.

Later we learned that two of the male revellers, both of them members of the naval contingent, ended up in the village of East

Rudham just a few miles west of Sculthorpe. One of them broke down the front door of an elderly female resident for some unknown reason, although alcohol certainly played a part. The police were summoned and the miscreant was arrested and taken to the police station in Fakenham where he was placed in a cell. Shortly afterwards, one of his sober and more responsible compatriots, a USAF Tech. Sergeant, got wind of the incident, and went to the police station to try to sort things out. The station police sergeant, probably not unaccustomed to the occasional revelling American serviceman when Sculthorpe was fully operational as a USAF base, informed the Tech. Sergeant that he would telephone the base at Lakenheath and have the US Air Force Police take care of the situation. The Tech. Sergeant hastily begged the police officer not to do that, informing him that he and his jailed colleague were part of a "special program," but asked that he be allowed to contact Commander Tyson instead. The police officer kindly consented to the Tech. Sergeant's request.

Commander Tyson soon showed up, accompanied by SCPO Roby, and managed to secure the release of the errant sailor on condition that he appear before the Fakenham magistrates' court soon afterwards. At the hearing, both Commander Tyson and Wing Commander Scrimgeour were obliged to attend as character witnesses. The sailor was sternly admonished for his behaviour and for the damage and distress he had caused, but got off lightly by only having to pay restitution to the woman for the damage to her door.

***

There were a few attempts by some on the American side to bridge the social gap. On one occasion, the RAF and GAF NCOs and airmen, together with our wives, were invited as guests of our American counterparts for a Saturday evening at Lakenheath NCOs' Club. Each member of the RAF group and his wife was "adopted" by one of our American colleagues, who met us and took us under his wing when the chartered coach delivered us to the club's front door. USAF Staff Sgt. Ernie Burn, our host for the evening, guided Pam and me, together with Dave King and his wife, into a large, low-ceilinged room with subdued, concealed lighting. A raised platform that served as a band stage and a parquet-wood dance floor occupied one quadrant of the room. Booth-type seating, reminiscent of that seen in posh American nightclubs depicted in the Hollywood films of that era, was arrayed around the periphery of the remaining wall space. Pam and I were seated in one of the plush semi-circular booths, together with our friends Dave King and his wife, and were invited to order a meal, which turned out to be a delicious prime rib steak dinner, made more enjoyable by indulging it in such a wonderful nightclub setting. Until then, neither Pam nor I had ever enjoyed such opulence. Ernie came back to check on us periodically, enough to be attentive, but not so much as to overdo his role of "host." The floorshow featured a number of high quality acts, one of which was a magician that I had previously seen on the then popular British TV show, *Sunday Night at the London Palladium*. After the floorshow finished, couples danced to a top-notch live band that played for remainder of the evening. Dinner was on the Americans although it was understandable that we had to pay for our own alcoholic drinks. Possibly, the RAF Senior NCOs reciprocated the Americans' generous gesture at another time, but being of very junior in rank at the time, I was unaware if that actually happened.

Another time, M/Sgt. Jones went to a lot of trouble to organize the establishment of a families' club in one of the wooden buildings that comprised the former Sculthorpe Base medical centre. He called a meeting on the premises to which all "married patch" denizens were invited. Jones' plan was a little on the ambitious side. He talked of persuading outside food and beverage companies to sponsor the club in return for the right to prominently advertise their sponsorship, as is done on American bases. Someone should have told him that neither the NAAFI (Navy, Army and Air Force Institute) nor MOD would ever agree to such a proposal, but no one did. We just let him ramble on. To his credit, the club did open, although more along the lines of a traditional RAF families club than an American one.

Our three nations represented by Arnold "Stew" Stewart (USAF), Phil May (RAF) and Günter Findiesen (GAF) pictured in front of the squadron hangar.
(Photo courtesy of Günter Findiesen)

WORKING WITH THE AMERICANS

Kestrel XS 694's maintenance crew posing in front of "their" aircraft. L to R, Günter Findiesen (GAF), Arnold "Stew" Stewart (USAF) and Dennis "Bonny" Boniface (RAF - recently promoted to Sergeant in this photo). *(Photo courtesy of Günter Findiesen)*

Col. Barkhorn climbing into the cockpit of XS 689, assisted by PO/1 Staffanson (USN) (Photo courtesy of Günter Findiesen).

WORKING WITH THE AMERICANS 85

Kestrel Squadron group at the NCO Club, Lakenheath.
L to R; Joe Crupi (US Army), Bill Heim (USAF), Glen Adair (US Army), Chris Hannan-Bobe (RAF), Angela May, Phil Smith (RAF), Phil May (RAF), Don Grunwell (RAF), Dieter Zinndorf (GAF). *Photo courtesy of Bonny Boniface*

Chapter 9: *A Hurricane and Another Kind of Kestrel*

One Friday afternoon during the summer of 1965, word got around that Bill Bedford, Hawker Siddeley's chief test pilot, would fly up from Dunsfold that day in the newly refurbished Hurricane, *"Last of Many,"* for a visit to the squadron. Airfield operations had ended for the week so there were no other air movements taking place. Work in the hangar and sections gradually came to stop, and squadron members began to congregate on the airfield side of the hangar as the news of the visit percolated around. Phone calls from the control tower to the pilots' crew room, relayed to the squadron at large, kept us all updated on the Hurricane's ETA. When it was very close, eyes and ears strained to catch a glimpse or hear the unmistakeable growl of its Merlin engine. The anticipated sound eventually reached our ears, although the fighter was nowhere to be seen. As the Merlin's husky voice grew louder and louder, heads swivelled around searching in all directions for a visual. As we looked high in the sky to unite the Hurricane with its disembodied engine sound, it startled everyone by sneaking in at low level for a high-speed pass right in front of the hangar. What then followed was the most exciting display of airmanship I have ever seen. Bedford put the Hurricane through every conceivable aerobatic manoeuvre – at times flying high with loops and rolls, and other times flying so close to the ground that he appeared to be mere inches above the aircraft parking area fronting the hangar. Periodically, I tore my eyes away from the display to catch a glimpse of Colonel Barkhorn's reaction, always to find that he was smiling as he watched, obviously enjoying the show like the rest of us.

Although Mr. Bedford put the Hurricane through its paces for much longer than one could expect at an air show, the thrill-packed display still left us wanting more when he eventually brought it in to land on the section of the taxiway adjacent to our hangar. He taxied towards us and parked squarely in front of the hangar. No sooner had the Hurricane come to a halt, with its engine still idling and propeller rotating, than Colonel Barkhorn walked out and climbed onto the wing to peer down on Bedford and into the cockpit.

Bill Bedford had been a fighter pilot during the Second World War, and a Battle of Britain veteran to boot. Colonel Barkhorn also participated in the Battle of Britain but as a member of the opposing team, although he had not claimed any victories in that particular campaign. This wasn't the first time that he and Bill Bedford had met, because the Colonel had already been to the Dunsfold factory on a Kestrel pilots' ground course and conversion training. In any event, although having been on opposite sides during the war, they had a lot in common as fighter pilots and had become good friends.

Barkhorn smiled as Bedford cut the fuel and the engine stuttered to a stop. Many of us had followed the Colonel out to the Hurricane and watched as he remained standing on the wing while Bill Bedford pointed out various things of interest within the cockpit. Finally, the Colonel climbed down, allowing Bedford to exit the cockpit. Someone shouted, "What do you think of it?" to the good-natured colonel. He smiled and replied, "Oh, it's very nice, but it has the wrong markings."

Bill Bedford spent a few hours with us but, as early evening approached, he climbed back into the Hurricane and after one last low-level, high-speed flypast with wings waving, he departed for Dunsfold. The Hurricane soon became a small dot in the sky before finally vanishing, but the memory of its visit to West Raynham that fine summer afternoon will stay with me forever.

* * *

On 30 September 1965, the squadron held a Press Day. Journalists from all the major British newspapers were invited to a demonstration of the Kestrel, (which they insisted on calling a "Jump-Jet"). During the visit, many photographs were taken and pilots interviewed. The photos and write-ups appeared in all the papers next day. *The Times*, of course, treated the matter seriously, but typically, the *Daily Mirror* zeroed in on one particular RAF Pilot, Flight Lieutenant Edmonston, who displayed his pet Kestrel hawk, which was the squadron mascot. Not only did Edmonston have the mascot, but he also sported a stereotypical RAF handlebar moustache. The *Mirror* made a big thing of his facial decoration, asking its readers, tongue in

A HURRICANE AND ANOTHER KIND OF KESTREL

cheek, to "spot" the RAF pilot within a group of four pilots – two of whom were Americans and the other a German. In the newspaper clipping, reproduced below, Flight Lieutenant Edmonston holds his Kestrel hawk aloft.

Flight Lieutenant Edmonston had owned the hawk since the early days of the squadron and he could often be seen on the grassy area in front of the hangar training it in the ancient art of falconry. The bird, hooded much of the time, perched on his gauntleted left hand, restrained from flying off by the leather thongs around its legs, which were gripped by the fingers of the gauntlet. Edmonston fed the Kestrel small snacks of raw meat so that it would associate his gauntleted hand with food rewards. As training progressed, the bird was allowed to fly free and then summoned to the gauntlet for its reward. Later, Edmonston whirled a lure around his head for the hawk to home in on and attack. The lure was a weighted piece of leather on a six feet length of line that had a meat snack firmly attached to the lure end. The bird was released and sent aloft, where it sometimes circled and other times hovered as it waited until the lure was whirled. Once the lure was in motion, it swooped down and grabbed it with its talons, bringing it to the ground to devour the small piece of meat. I'm sure that later on, Flight Lieutenant Edmonston probably advanced the bird's education by having it attack real birds, but that never happened on the squadron grounds.

Edmonston was well known amongst groundcrew members for one other minor idiosyncrasy. When strapping into the ejection seat for a sortie, he would go around each of the seat straps in turn, cinching them so tight that it seemed they would cut off the blood supply to his arms and legs. On one occasion, a groundcrew member, who was helping him to strap in, casually asked why he went to such an extreme when other pilots simply made sure the seat straps were firmly tight, but not uncomfortably so. Edmonston confided that, as a fighter pilot, he had racked up many flying hours in Hunters and had been obliged to eject on one particular sortie. The experience taught him that being securely strapped into the seat was essential to avoid lower back injuries. The prospect of suddenly being accelerated from the aircraft in this new type of seat, propelled by a powerful rocket pack, only reinforced his determination to be as securely strapped in as was humanly bearable.

***

After what had seemed an age, my promotion to corporal finally came through. On receiving the good news, I made a beeline for the clothing store to collect my brand new corporal chevrons. Pam sewed them onto my working blue that evening so that I could display my newly exalted status at work next day. When I arrived in the E&I Section in the morning, there were congratulations all round. It was a good feeling, but I felt bad for my colleague, Dave Thornley because he was now the sole RAF Junior Technician in the section.

***

As time passed, Dieter Zinndorf's command of English improved to the point of being completely fluent, and both he and his fellow German, Günter Findiesen, turned out to be good friends.

One day, Deiter arrived at work in a brand new, green Triumph Spitfire sports car. What could the rest of us do but pull his leg unmercifully? Cries of "Achtung, Spitfeuer!" rang out more than once when he was seen driving it, but he took it all in good spirits and really enjoyed driving his Spitfeuer. His good-natured attitude towards our leg pulling certainly contradicted the conventional wisdom that Germans don't have much sense of humour.

Spot the man from the RAF

ONLY one of the four pilots above is British. Can you spot him?

That's right, the chap with the bang-on moustache—Flight-Lieutenant David Edmonston of the RAF.

With him, admiring their feathered mascot yesterday, are (from the left): Flight-Lt. V. Suhr (Germany), and Majors J. K. Campbell and John Johnston (America).

They belong to the world's most exclusive squadron formed a year ago to fly the British jump-jet, the Kestrel.

Britain, America and Germany are sharing the cost of developing the jet. Yesterday the pilots demonstrated the Kestrels at RAF Bircham Newton, Norfolk.

Then they showed off their mascot—a kestrel, of course.

(Daily Mirror clipping dated 1st October, 1965.)

92 KESTREL SQUADRON

The "Last of Many" Hurricane pays a visit to the squadron. Pilot Bill Bedford (centre) chats with Sqdn. Ldr. Trowern (left) and 1st Lt. Suhr (right).
(Photo courtesy of Bonny Boniface)

Chapter 10: The Squadron Disbands

On the 30th of November 1965, the flying part of the trials came to an end, although several more weeks would pass before the squadron itself disbanded. Reports had to be written up, while many other activities associated with the squadron disbandment needed to be performed. One of these was the division of the aircraft between participating nations.

Each government was entitled to three Kestrels, per the original agreement, but because of the loss of XS686, there were now only eight aircraft to consider. The West German government had been lukewarm about the whole concept of the trials, as reflected in the token number of GAF personnel they had assigned to the squadron and the smaller proportion of funding it contributed to the evaluation squadron. Germany therefore decided that it was only interested in the Pegasus engine because, at that time, it was developing the Dornier Do 31, a VTOL military transport aircraft that employed two Pegasus engines for its forward thrust and eight Rolls-Royce RB162 engines for the vertical lift component. The Americans, on the other hand, were very interested in the aircraft, so they traded some of their Pegasus engines for the German share of Kestrels. As a result, the Americans received six aircraft, including XS689, which had been repaired at the Hawker Siddeley factory after its heavy landing damage. On taking possession of the aircraft allotted to them, they renamed them the "XV-6A Kestrel." The XV-6As were then used in further trials in the United States, which is discussed in more detail later. Today, a number of the XV-6A Kestrels still survive in various American air museums.

The RAF ended up with just two aircraft, XS693 and XS695. The latter (No. 5), after having experienced a chequered post-Kestrel Evaluation Squadron history, including several undignified roles, happily ended up being restored, and is currently on display at the Royal Air Force Museum Cosford in its Kestrel Squadron livery.

Sadly, XS693 was lost on 21 September 1967 whilst being flown from Filton airfield, near Bristol, to the Royal Aircraft Establishment airfield, Boscombe Down, on the edge of Salisbury Plain. On approach to runway 05, the engine developed a potentially damaging surge condition. In an attempt to correct it, the pilot shut off the fuel supply. He then tried to restart the engine, but was unsuccessful. Now at a height of only 200 feet, there was insufficient altitude to reach the runway so his only option was to eject. The Kestrel crashed approximately one mile short of the runway, at an area known as High Post, not very far from Stonehenge. Happily, the pilot survived the incident, thanks in no small measure to the rocket-assisted ejection seat that proved itself that day.

***

During the next few months, squadron members went about the business of disposing of equipment, spare parts, tools and other miscellaneous items that had been part of our lives for the past two years. The Kestrels were flown back to Dunsfold, where those bound for America were dissembled and crated for ocean shipment.

In addition to the six Kestrels being shipped to America, other less official cargo was also included. Several Americans; USAF Tech. Sgt. Chuck Massey, USAF Staff Sgt. Art Snyder, US Army Specialists Joe Crupi and Glen Adair, USN Ch. P.O. Doug Lynn and USN P.O. John Staffanson had all purchased new VW beetle cars during their time on the squadron and had them shipped home to America, taking advantage of the tax-free concession they were allowed. In the same vein, P.O. James Osbourn fell in love with a British Mk. 1 Ford Cortina he had bought while on Kestrel Squadron, so he also arranged for it to be sent to the US. Major Curry had acquired an older car, possibly a Bentley, which was in need of a lot of restoration work, so his purchase was despatched to the States as well.

In the midst of saying goodbye to our international partners as they departed for their own countries, there was some loose-end paperwork for RAF personnel to finalize. Because of his association with TSTS (Trade Standards & Testing Squadron), one of Chief Tech. Meek's tasks on the squadron had been to keep careful notes of maintenance issues that could eventually be used by Trade Standards to produce servicing manuals, should the Kestrel go into subsequent service. To this end, he sought input from others. My contribution was reminding him of the need to cut a hole in the fuselage for fuel pressure switch access, which was duly noted. This and other problems that we found in the course of our servicing duties were documented and, I believe, subsequently incorporated into the Harrier design. For instance, we discovered that because the battery compartment was located very close to the rear hot jet nozzles, serious battery overheating resulted. I recall that this was corrected by force-ventilating the compartment on the early Harriers, and possibly moving the batteries to another location in later versions.

It was then time for us to be posted to other stations, although one person that I'm aware of, my friend Dave King, who worked in the squadron store, remained at West Raynham, having been transferred to the station's main store. For me, it was back to Bomber Command and Vulcans, with an effective posting date of 1st of February 1966. However, my posting was to Scampton instead of Waddington, where I would have preferred to return. Also posted to Scampton was my electrical fitter colleague J/T Dave Thornley.

A typical 1965 Model Mk.1 Ford Cortina

THE SQUADRON DISBANDS 97

Four Kestrels in line abreast formation.
(Squadron publicity photo)

Chapter 11: Kestrel Squadron Aftermath

The American contingent of Kestrel Squadron remained together as a unit on repatriation to the United States, with the U.S. Army remaining in charge. The unit was headquartered at Fort Campbell in Kentucky. A series of national trials of the aircraft, now renamed the XV-6A, were performed at Fort Campbell, at Naval Air Test Center Patuxent River including on Navy ships and at Eglin Air Force Base in Florida.

Commander Jim Tyson, USN, one of the two deputy commanders of Kestrel Squadron, led the U.S. Navy's portion of the trials. The following is a description of the Navy's trials, in Tyson's own words. (Missing words and clarifications have been inserted in italics by the author).

"Preparations and work-up for shipboard evaluations *were* done at the U.S. Naval Air Test Center, Patuxent River, MD, in May 1966. With four XV-6A (P.1127, Kestrel) airplanes, a group of pilots flew them aboard USS Independence (CVA-62). Five qualified pilots were assigned at the time. FRG (*Federal Republic of Germany*) Colonel Barkhorn "walked aboard" *the Independence* while the four U.S. pilots flew the initial flight to the ship. Colonel Barkhorn took the first flight *off the USS Independence* afterwards…The ship was at anchor in Hampton Roads during the initial flights aboard.

"In my opinion, these were not 'firsts' because Chief Test Pilot Bill Bedford of Hawker Aircraft had made landings on a British aircraft carrier, HMS Ark Royal, in 1961 using one of the P.1127 test vehicles from which the Kestrel was developed.

"Daytime test flights of the XV-6A were made by all pilots during the following days while the ship was *both* at anchor and underway. Operations were mixed with normal operation of standard fixed-wing airplanes as well as operations when the ship was "out of the wind," i.e. not launching or receiving its regular airplanes. No problems were encountered. Our operations were similar to those in use today by USMC for their AV-8Bs and F-35Bs on board the large-deck vessels designated for combined operations, LHD/LHA/LPD (*Landing*

Helicopter Dock/Amphibious Assault Ship/Amphibious Transport Dock), etc.

"Follow-on tests for the XV-6A use aboard a ship assigned to the amphibious landing fleet were conducted in the Hampton Roads area. I (*Commander Tyson*) made the first landing/takeoff on such a ship, USS Raleigh (LPD-1), *which is* not an 'aircraft carrier' as commonly described. It was at anchor. The LPD was configured with a helicopter landing area on the after-part of the ship. All landings and takeoffs were, of necessity, vertical. Thus the range and endurance of the airplane was restricted...Flights were made while the ship was at anchor and underway, up to 17 knots of wind from dead ahead. I (*Commander Tyson*) claim the 'first' landing of a fixed-wing jet airplane on a ship not defined as an 'aircraft carrier.' Fuel considerations limited *the* flights to about 20 minutes each, with only one shipboard landing/takeoff per sortie. Modern VSTOL airplanes have more powerful engines, giving them better vertical performance."

The USAF trials were held at Edwards AFB and Point Magoo AFB, in addition to Eglin AFB. Details of these trials are sketchy, but it is known that one of the aircraft, USAF serial number 64-18264 (formerly XS690) was mounted on a test stand at Edwards AFB for two weeks, during December 1967, and extensive tests of the engine thrust parameters were carried out with the nozzles in various angles. A feature of the test stand was that it could be raised and lowered hydraulically. This enabled the mounting frame to be attached to the underside of the aircraft when it was at ground level. The hydraulic lift feature also made it possible for the operator to climb into the cockpit before the Kestrel was raised high enough for the thrust measurements to be unaffected by the "ground effect" during the testing.

***

America's involvement in the Vietnam War was escalating at that time, so it's reasonable to assume that several US personnel with whom I had worked ended up there. As for the squadron's three leading officers; Wing Commander David Scrimgeour, RAF; Commander Jim Tyson, USN; and Colonel Barkhorn, GAF all went on to expand their careers in different directions.

After the Kestrel Evaluation Squadron trials, **Wing Commander David Scrimgeour** visited America to brief members of the USAF and US Navy staff on VSTOL techniques. Following this, he participated in duties connected with the introduction of the Harrier into RAF service, before becoming Station Commander of RAF Wildenrath, Germany, just as the first Harriers to be based in that country were arriving. He eventually retired from the RAF in 1982, having achieved the rank of Air Commodore. Besides being Commanding Officer of the Kestrel Evaluation Squadron, David Scrimgeour is also remembered for his post-Kestrel Squadron work in developing off-base dispersal techniques that became the initial standard operational procedures for the Harrier Force.

***

Following his work with the XV-6A, **Commander Jim Tyson** returned to more conventional aircraft. He took command of an A4 Skyhawk attack squadron on the aircraft carrier USS Coral Sea, from which he saw action in the skies over Vietnam. An extract from his biography featured on the *Osher Lifelong Learning Institute at UNC Asheville (OLLI)* website, and reproduced here by kind permission of the Osher Lifelong Learning Institute at UNC Asheville (OLLI), reads:

"Following a night launch from the USS Coral Sea in the Gulf of Tonkin, in 1968, Jim started a radar bombing run at 20,000 feet into Vietnam's DMZ.

"This 'trip' took me into every kind of weather I had ever heard of - monsoonal rain, lightning, hail, St. Elmo's fire! And this did not include the excitement caused by the enemy's weaponry lighting up the cockpit detection equipment."

He dropped his bombs then flew back through the same great weather only to execute a night carrier landing. Jim didn't see the carrier deck until six seconds before touchdown; he was less than 300 feet over the water!

He was promoted to the rank of Captain after holding a number of other appointments on the USS Coral Sea and took over as

Commander of an Attack Carrier Air Wing on the USS Enterprise before being assigned to the Pentagon for various other appointments.

Captain Tyson retired in 1977 after having served 30 years in the service, but he wasn't going out to grass that easily. Having settled with his wife and family in Asheville, North Carolina, he utilized his engineering degree by launching on a civilian career in project engineering and technical services. However, flying was always in his DNA, so not surprisingly, he purchased a single engine, 4-seat Grumman American Tiger, which he still flies. He has always been a "stick and rudder man," as he told me in a recent telephone conversation.

Captain Tyson has used his Tiger in conjunction with Angel Flight, a non-profit organization of pilots and other volunteers that provide free private air transportation for medical patients who cannot afford the cost of normal commercial airline travel.

Since 2004, he has also taught several courses, including 'The Evolution of Aircraft' and 'History of Aircraft Carriers,' as part of the Osher Lifelong Learning Institute's College for Seniors program at the University of North Carolina's Asheville campus, as well as serving on the Institute's Curriculum Committee.

Jim, now Captain Tyson USN (retired), kindly contributed some of the material included in this book.

***

Colonel (Oberst) Gerhard Barkhorn was involved briefly with the American trials of the Kestrel, as mentioned above. Then, in 1970, four years after the disbandment of the Kestrel Evaluation Squadron, he was promoted to the rank of Brigadier General (Brigadegeneral) in the German Air Force and subsequently, in 1973, to Major General (Generalmajor). His final appointment was to Chief of Staff of NATO's 2ATAF (Second Allied Tactical Air Force) in Germany before retiring from active service in 1975. Ironically, despite his daredevil prowess as a fighter pilot, "The Colonel" lost his life on January 1983 in a car accident on the German autobahn near Cologne

during a winter storm. The accident also claimed the life of his wife Christi.
Source: Wikipedia

***

Flight Lieutenant Tony "Porky" Munro's immediate post Kestrel Squadron history is a little obscure, but it seems that he may have spent time on 79 (FR) Squadron and was later instrumental in compiling the first Harrier "Pilot Notes" (a manual specific to a particular type of aircraft that provides the pilot with the information needed to safely operate it). It is possible that he joined Number 1 Squadron, RAF, since it was the first squadron to be equipped with Harriers, although that didn't occur until 1969, two years after the disbandment of Kestrel Squadron.

Some time later, around 1976, Porky was stationed in the Persian Gulf Sultanate of Oman where he was a Squadron Leader in charge of Fighter Operations. At this time, he may have been retired from the RAF and was then a member of the SOFA (Sultan of Oman's Air Force, later to become the Royal Air Force of Oman, RAFO). In this context he is mentioned by Rod Dean in his book, *Fifty Years of Flying Fun*, when, in 1982, he was waiting to meet Rod and others as they taxied in after participating in a Hawker Hunter display formation. On dismounting, Rod and two other members of the display team were invited to Porky's office where he then proceeded to "bollock" them because Dean had participated in the formation without proper authorization. However, it seems that the bollocking was more tongue-in-cheek in nature than severe.

Porky eventually achieved the rank of Group Captain as Director of Operations at the RAFO Headquarters, but was forced to retire back to the UK when he suffered a severe stroke. He made a good recovery from the stroke and survived it by several years.

***

USAF Tech. Sgt Charles "Chuck" Massey was assigned to assist with the USAF's own assessment of Kestrels in the United States, together with George Irgens, Arnold L. "Stew" Stewart, Harvey

West and Art Snyder. Chuck remained with the USAF Kestrel trials for a longer period than any of his Air Force colleagues and accompanied the Kestrel, or AV-6A as it was now known, to Edwards and Point Magoo Air Force bases (both in California) and to Eglin AFB in Florida. On retirement, Chuck returned to his native Texas. When I spoke with Chuck recently at his home in Burleson (near Dallas), he informed me that he is the last surviving member of the Kestrel Squadron USAF team. Chuck kindly contributed some of the material included in this book.

***

RAF Sgt. Dennis "Bonny" Boniface, with whom I have corresponded extensively during the compilation of this book and who has contributed much of the source material, remained in the RAF until 1985. He and his wife Lin now own a smallholding in southwest Shropshire where, on about 3 acres of grass paddocks and stables, they enjoy keeping Lin's horses.

Bonny actually built the house on the property in which he and Lin now reside. He credits his RAF boy entrant training and subsequent RAF experience in taking on the property and teaching himself how to go about the job of house-building. (We can only surmise what M/Sgt. Jones would have had to say about that). The rural location also complements his other passion; bird watching. Daily, he sees buzzards, red kites nuthatches, thrushes and many other feathered members of the bird kingdom.

Bonny and I renewed our acquaintance when we met again after 50 years, at the Newark Air Museum, Newark, Nottinghamshire, England, in June 2016.

***

Feldwebel Günter Findiesen of the German Air Force met his future wife while serving on the squadron. It all started when he became friends with RAF Sergeant Dave Young who was a fellow live-in member of the West Raynham Sergeants Mess. Dave occasionally invited Günter to spend the weekend with him at his mother's home in London. A result of this friendship was that Günter was introduced to

Dave's cousin Beryl, who was a nurse. It could all have ended when Dave was unexpectedly posted to Singapore, but by then Günter had formed a firm friendship with the family. Beryl offered to show him around the sights of London and through this, she and Günter became close friends. The friendship deepened into a courtship, which continued when Günter returned to Norvenich, Germany, after the Kestrel Squadron had disbanded. For a time, they communicated by letter-writing but eventually Beryl moved to Germany where she and Günter married on December 31, 1966. They have remained together ever since and recently celebrated their 50th wedding anniversary. Günter was later transferred to Koln-Porz airport, where he worked until retirement.

***

Junior Technician Dave King remained at RAF West Raynham after the disbandment of Kestrel Squadron and was reassigned to work in the station's Main Store. In 1966, he was promoted to the rank of Corporal and shortly thereafter was sent on a 1-year posting to RAF Muharraq on the island of Bahrain in the Persian Gulf. On his return, Dave was posted to RAF Watton in Norfolk, not too far from our old base of West Raynham.

In 1969, Dave resigned from the RAF and began working in the textile industry. Around this time, he met Sue and they married on Christmas Eve 1974. Dave also changed jobs and began working in the Touring Caravan industry, relocating to Soham, Cambridgeshire. After the arrival of their two children, Barry and Emma, the family moved to a larger property in Lakenheath, Suffolk, where they lived until 2011. That year, they moved to Mablethorpe on the Lincolnshire coast where Dave retired from the Touring Caravan industry.

Daughter Emma married a USAF Chief Master Sergeant, became a U.S. citizen, and currently lives with her husband in Texas. Son Barry works for the British Ministry of Defence and lives on Suffolk. He has graced Dave and Sue with their only grandchild, Iris.

***

On returning to the United States, many of the U.S. Army and USAF enlisted personnel were awarded the United States Army Commendation Medal. A copy of the citation is reproduced on the next two pages, by courtesy of Chuck Massey. The U.S. Navy enlisted men may also have been awarded a similar medal, but this has not been confirmed.

GENERAL ORDERS)   HEADQUARTERS
                    DEPARTMENT OF THE ARMY
NO.   27)   Washington, D. C., 27 June 1966

EXTRACT

*   *   *   *   *

V. ARMY COMMENDATION MEDAL. 1. By direction of the Secretary of the Army, under the provisions of paragraph 33, AR 672-5-1, the Army Commendation Medal for meritorious service is awarded to:
    Specialist Five Glen E. Adair, RA19763009, United States Army. February 1965 to December 1965.

*   *   *   *   *

    Master Sergeant Buel N. Arbuckle, Jr., AF14627193, United States Air Force. November 1964 to December 1965.

*   *   *   *   *

    Technical Sergeant Ernest L. Burn, AF12323483, United States Air Force. December 1964 to December 1965.
    Specialist Five Clarence B. Canady, Jr., RA18299246, United States Army. December 1964 to January 1966.

*   *   *   *   *

    Specialist Six Joseph R. Crupi, RA12461380, United States Army. December 1964 to February 1966.
    Specialist Five Curtis L. Darus, RA14416869, United States Army. February 1965 to December 1965.
    Specialist Five Mickey R. Davis, RA14630550, United States Army. December 1964 to January 1966.

*   *   *   *   *

    Master Sergeant Raymond A. Dix, RA22888439, United States Army. October 1964 to November 1965.
    Staff Sergeant William H. Elliott, RA25420561, United States Army. December 1964 to February 1966.

*   *   *   *   *

    Specialist Five Gerald C. Gipson, RA25553278, United States Army. April 1965 to December 1965.

*   *   *   *   *

    Master Sergeant William B. Heim, AF15228392, United States Air Force. November 1964 to February 1966.
    Specialist Six Larry C. Hill, RA16563643, United States Army. May 1965 to December 1965.
    Senior Master Sergeant George T. Irgens, AF19015516, United States Air Force. October 1964 to February 1966.

*   *   *   *   *

    Technical Sergeant Charles G. Massey, AF18421931, United States Air Force. December 1964 to February 1966.

*   *   *   *   *

Extract of General Orders No. 27 (Cont'd)   27 Jun 66

    Staff Sergeant Gerald A. Minor, RA11205670, United States Army. November 1964 to January 1966.

*   *   *   *   *

    Sergeant First Class Charles A. Perry, RA14166124, United States Army. December 1964 to December 1965.
    Specialist Five Herbert E. Pettiford, RA13697802, United States Army. April 1965 to January 1966.
    Technical Sergeant William G. Pinto, Jr., AF18503339, United States Air Force. December 1964 to December 1965.

*   *   *   *   *

    Senior Master Sergeant James W. Prines, AF15413535, United States Air Force. October 1964 to February 1966.

*   *   *   *   *

    Technical Sergeant Arthur D. Snyder, AF17329654, United States Air Force. December 1964 to February 1966.
    Specialist Five Robert S. Steiner, RA13751891, United States Army. October 1964 to January 1966.
    Technical Sergeant Arnold L. Stewart, AF18537884, United States Air Force. December 1964 to February 1966.
    Specialist Six John H. Surbrook, RA19509146, United States Army. December 1964 to December 1965.

*   *   *   *   *

    Lieutenant Colonel Joel T. Wareing, FR38925, United States Air Force. January 1962 to February 1966.
    Technical Sergeant Harvey L. West, AF14448514, United States Air Force. December 1964 to December 1965.

*   *   *   *   *

By Order of the Secretary of the Army:

HAROLD K. JOHNSON,
General, United States Army,
Chief of Staff.

Official:
J. C. LAMBERT,
Major General, United States Army,
The Adjutant General.

A TRUE EXTRACT COPY:

[signature: Walter E. Coleman]
WALTER E. COLEMAN
Lt Colonel, GS
Asst Exec for Administration

The RAF "other ranks" personnel did not receive any such recognition by the British authorities for our participation in the evaluation of this historic aircraft, nor did we expect any. We were simply doing our job and, in my humble opinion, it was a job well done.

***

On 28 December 1967, an uprated production version of Kestrel, renamed the Harrier, had its first flight. It then went into service with the RAF on 1 April 1969. Later, a marine version went into service with the Royal Navy. Ironically, the US Marine Corps, the sole American branch of the military that did not participate in the Tripartite Kestrel Evaluation Squadron, was the only American service that foresaw the usefulness of this unique aircraft in support of its mission.

After some involvement in the trials in the United States, the Marines took up the option of ordering Harriers, renaming it the AV-8A. Later, McDonnell-Douglas obtained licensing from Hawker Siddeley to manufacture an improved version in the USA, which was given the designation AV-8B. The USMC is still using Harriers to this day, although the current version is scheduled to be replaced in the near future by the Lockheed Martin F-35 Lightning.

The four pilots who flew the XV-6A Kestrels onto the USS Independence. (Second from the left) - Mjr. John Johnson (US Army), on his right - Cmdr. Jim Tyson (USN), Mjr. Paul Curry (US Army) and Mjr. J.K. Campbell (USAF) with trademark cigar held between the fingers of his right hand.
Col. Barkhorn (GAF) is on the extreme left of the group and Mjr. Bill King (US Army), on the extreme right.
(Mjr. King was the Kestrel Squadron Maintenance Officer. Although a pilot in his own right, he was not qualified to fly the XV-6A Kestrel).
(Photo : Naval Aviation News magazine, September 1966)

XS 690 (USAF 64-18264) on the raised test stand at Edwards Air Force Base.
(Photo: Northrop News, December 1967 via Chuck Massey)

Back row, standing – members of the disbanded Kestrel Squadron's USAF enlisted men contingent at Edwards AFB. Left to right: Snr. Master Sgt George Irgens, Staff Sgt. Stew Stewart, Tech. Sgt. Chuck Massey, Tech. Sgt. Harvey West, Staff Sgt. Art Snyder.
(Photo courtesy of Chuck Massey)

Dennis "Bonny" Boniface and author Brian Carlin meet again, 50 years after their service on Kestrel Squadron.

Günter Findiesen posing by the RAF Station West Raynham main gate
(Photo courtesy of Günter Findiesen)

Chapter 12: *The Fate of the Aircraft*

Nine P1127 Kestrels were built specifically for the Tripartite Kestrel Evaluation Squadron. One, XS696, was lost early in the evaluation and, of the remaining eight; two remained in Britain while the other six were shipped to the United States for further trials. The illustrations displayed on the following pages portray the present day disposition of all nine aircraft.

116 KESTREL SQUADRON

XS 688 *– Shipped to the United States under its USAF serial number 64-18262. Now on display in its USAF livery at Wright-Patterson Museum, Ohio.*
(Photo: courtesy of Wright-Patterson Museum)

THE FATE OF THE AIRCRAFT

XS 689 – *Shipped to the United States under its USAF serial number 64-18263. It was assigned to NASA and given serial number NASA 521. It is now on display at the Virginia Air & Space Museum in its NASA livery. (Photo; courtesy of Virginia Air & Space Museum)*

XS 690 – *Shipped to the United States under its USAF serial number 64-18264. It has been restored and is on display at Pima Air Museum, Tucson, Arizona, in its original Kestrel Squadron livery and serial number; but wearing a Harrier nose cone in place of its lost original.*
(Photo courtesy of Pima Air Museum)

THE FATE OF THE AIRCRAFT

119

XS 691 *– Shipped to the United States under its USAF serial number 64-18265 (nicknamed Cyclops 5). The numeral 5 on the nose relates to its USAF serial number; 64-18265. It participated in the USAF trials at Edwards AFB before being broken up and scrapped there in 1970.*

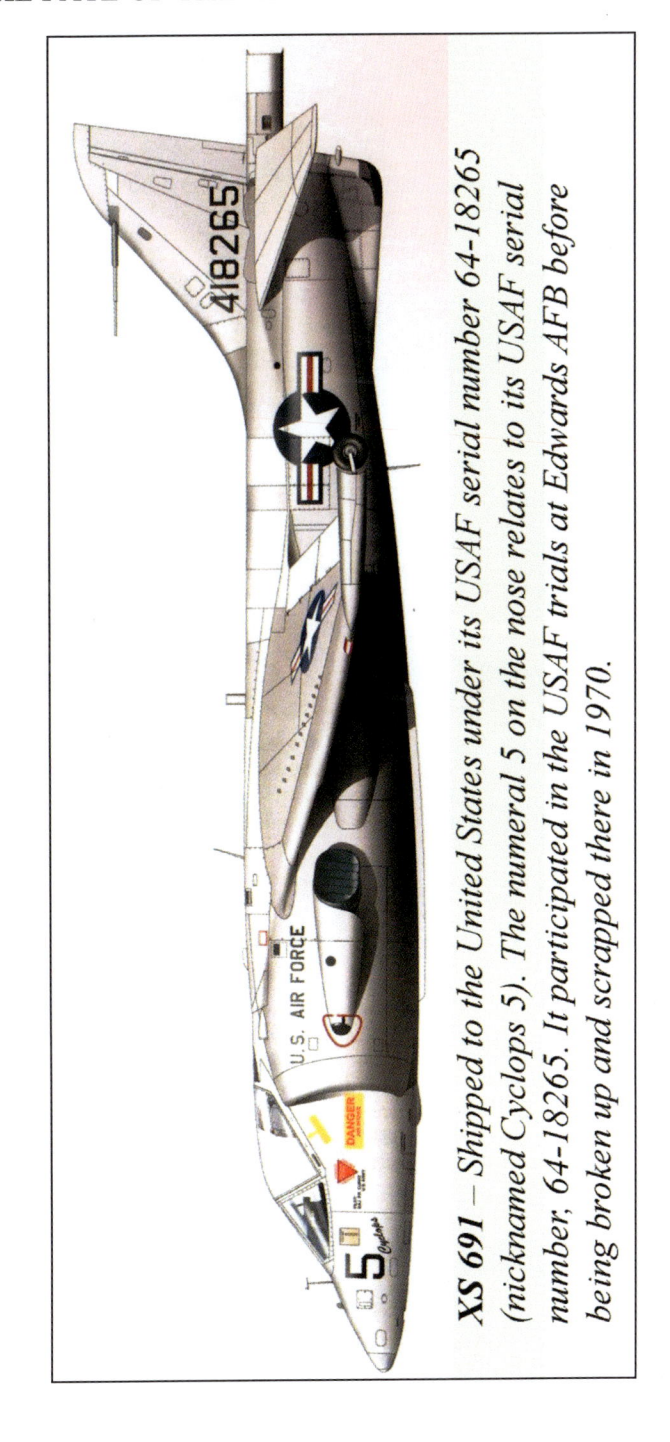

XS 692 - Shipped to the United States under its USAF serial number 6-18266. It too was assigned to NASA and given serial number NASA 520. It is now on display at Air Power Park, Hampton, Virginia in its NASA livery.
(Photo: courtesy of Air Power Park Museum)

THE FATE OF THE AIRCRAFT

XS 693 – Remained in the UK even though it had been assigned USAF serial number 64-18267. It was used for research by the Royal Aircraft Establishment, but was lost when it crashed on approach to Boscombe Down on September 21, 1967. The pilot ejected and survived the incident.

XS 694 – Shipped to the United States under its USAF serial number 64-18268. After completion of the U.S. trials, the Kestrel found a home at an Orlando, Florida air museum. Sometime later, it turned up in a paintball park in Pennsylvania, where it suffered abuse and vandalism. In 2009, a private individual with an interest in Vietnam War era helicopters discovered it at the paintball park and purchased it. He transported it to his farm in Connecticut, where it presently resides. The owner has stated that he is willing to part with it if any aviation museum or collector is interested.
(Photo: courtesy of Bob Parker)

THE FATE OF THE AIRCRAFT

123

XS 695 – Remained in the UK eventually being acquired by the RAF Cosford Air Museum, where it was restored to its original condition and livery. (Photo by Bonny Boniface)

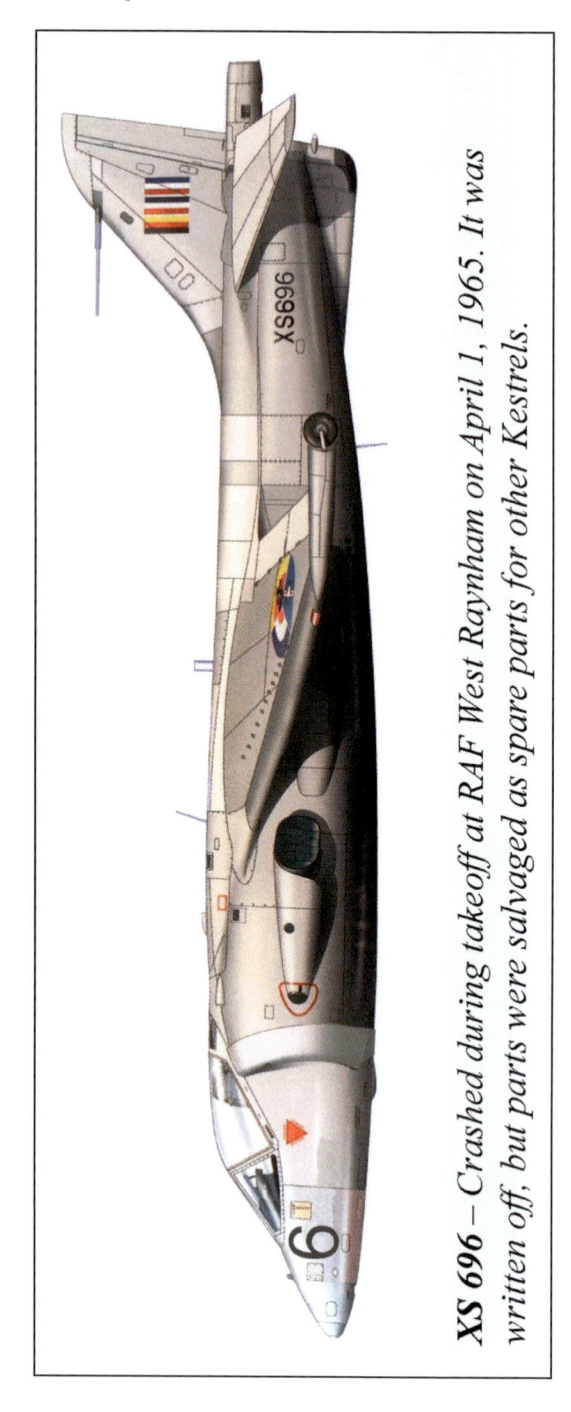

XS 696 – Crashed during takeoff at RAF West Raynham on April 1, 1965. It was written off, but parts were salvaged as spare parts for other Kestrels.

THE FATE OF THE AIRCRAFT

Hurricane PZ865, The Last of Many, appeared in the film, "Battle of Britain" and was eventually donated to the RAF Battle of Britain Memorial Flight by Hawker Siddeley.

Chapter 13: About the Author

Born in Coleraine, Northern Ireland in February 1941, I joined the Royal Air Force as a boy entrant in October 1956 to train as an aircraft electrician, four months prior to my sixteenth birthday. For the next 18 months, I underwent the rigours of military and technical training, (as related in my book, *Boy Entrant*, available on Amazon), graduating in the closing days of March 1958. I was then posted to the Royal Air Force College Cranwell (Flying Training Command), but still being underage, remained in the rank of Boy Entrant until reaching the age of 17-1/2 when my promotion to the rank of Leading Aircraftsman (LAC) became effective. During the next four years at Cranwell, I was engaged in servicing Vampires, Meteors, Jet Provosts and Chipmunks.

In April 1962, and now with the rank of Junior Technician, I was selected to participate in RAF's trials of the American made Skybolt air-launched ballistic missile with which the Vulcan V-bomber was to be armed. The trials were to be held at the USAF Eglin Air Force Base in Florida. In order to gain familiarization with the Vulcan, I was attached to Bomber Command's 230 Operational Conversion Unit at RAF Finningly, Yorkshire.

Unfortunately for me, the U.S. Government cancelled the Skybolt programme in December, which meant that the trials were also cancelled. Therefore, instead of going to sunny Florida, I went instead to Bomber Command station RAF Waddington in March 1963 to serve on 50 Squadron, which was equipped with Vulcans. In June 1964, while still at Waddington, my fiancée Pam and I were married. A short time later, in October, I was selected to participate in the Kestrel Tripartite Evaluation Squadron, the subject of this book.

At the conclusion of the Kestrel Evaluation Trials, I returned to Bomber Command and the Vulcans, but this time it was to RAF Scampton, with an official posting date of 1st February 1966. Once again, however, October seemed to be a fateful month because I was posted overseas to RAF Labuan, located on an island offshore the Malaysian part of Borneo. Because my tour at Labuan was "unaccompanied," I sadly had to go there without Pam, but two months later the posting was changed to RAF Changi in Singapore and my tour converted to "accompanied." A short time later, Pam joined me and we set up home in a rented apartment in the Katong district of Singapore.

Repatriation to the UK occurred in August 1968, with a posting back to RAF Scampton, where I served out the remainder of my time in the RAF, attaining the rank of Sergeant before becoming a plain, civilian "Mr." on 16th of February 1971. I then accepted the position of Electrical Draughtsman at Ruston Gas Turbines Ltd, based in the City of Lincoln, eventually gaining promotion to the position of Electrical Applications Engineer.

While my position as an Electrical Applications Engineer was professionally rewarding, the remuneration that Ruston paid was not. It became all the more acute because we were now a family of four - our two daughters Michelle and Sarah arriving in 1971 and 1973 respectively. Therefore, in 1977, the prospect of better financial reward lured me into signing up for a one-year contract with the Arabian American Oil Company (ARAMCO). This was for employment as a Project Engineer for the SCECO (Saudi Consolidated Electric Company) an offshoot of ARAMCO, which was tasked by the Saudi government with the electrification of the Eastern Province. My major project was the installation of a mobile generator station with underground utilities in the small desert town of Quaryat Al Ulya, approximately 200 miles northwest of ARAMCO's Dharan headquarters. Once again, I found myself working closely with Americans since all of my supervisors and most other fellow engineers were American. Also, just like my RAF "unaccompanied" overseas posting to Labuan, the contract was "bachelor status," except that this time it meant separation from Pam and the children for a whole year, but I did get to come home on leave every three months.

On returning to Lincoln and the family, my old firm, Ruston, offered me a position at their Houston, Texas, branch, Ruston Gas Turbines Inc., which I readily accepted. At first, we only intended to stay for one year to see how it was, but after a few months ion the United States, we realized that we could not go back to our old life in Britain, believing that America offered the best chances for our daughters. One year later, we began the frustrating and lengthy process of obtaining permanent resident "green card" status. Achieving this freed me to work for any company in the United States and not be tied to Ruston by the bonds of a temporary work visa.

ABOUT THE AUTHOR

In 1981, I received an offer of employment as a Project Engineer from Solar Turbines Incorporated, which I accepted. Initially, this was in their Houston office, but in 1985, the company transferred me to its home base in San Diego, California, with promotion to project manager. In May 1992, we all became American citizens.

I remained with Solar Turbines for a total of 19 years before retiring in the year 2000 from the position of Principal Project Manager. After retiring, I began a small consulting business catering exclusively to my former employer, which brings us up to the present time. I am content to live out my days in San Diego where our two daughters and five grandchildren also reside.

Not the final word.
This book is a compilation of my personal memories and those of a few other former squadron members, coupled with a fair amount of research. If anyone reading this also served on Kestrel Squadron, or knows someone who did, their contribution to a future edition would be welcome. Please feel free to contact me at my email address brian.carlin29@gmail.com. Comments on the book are also welcome.

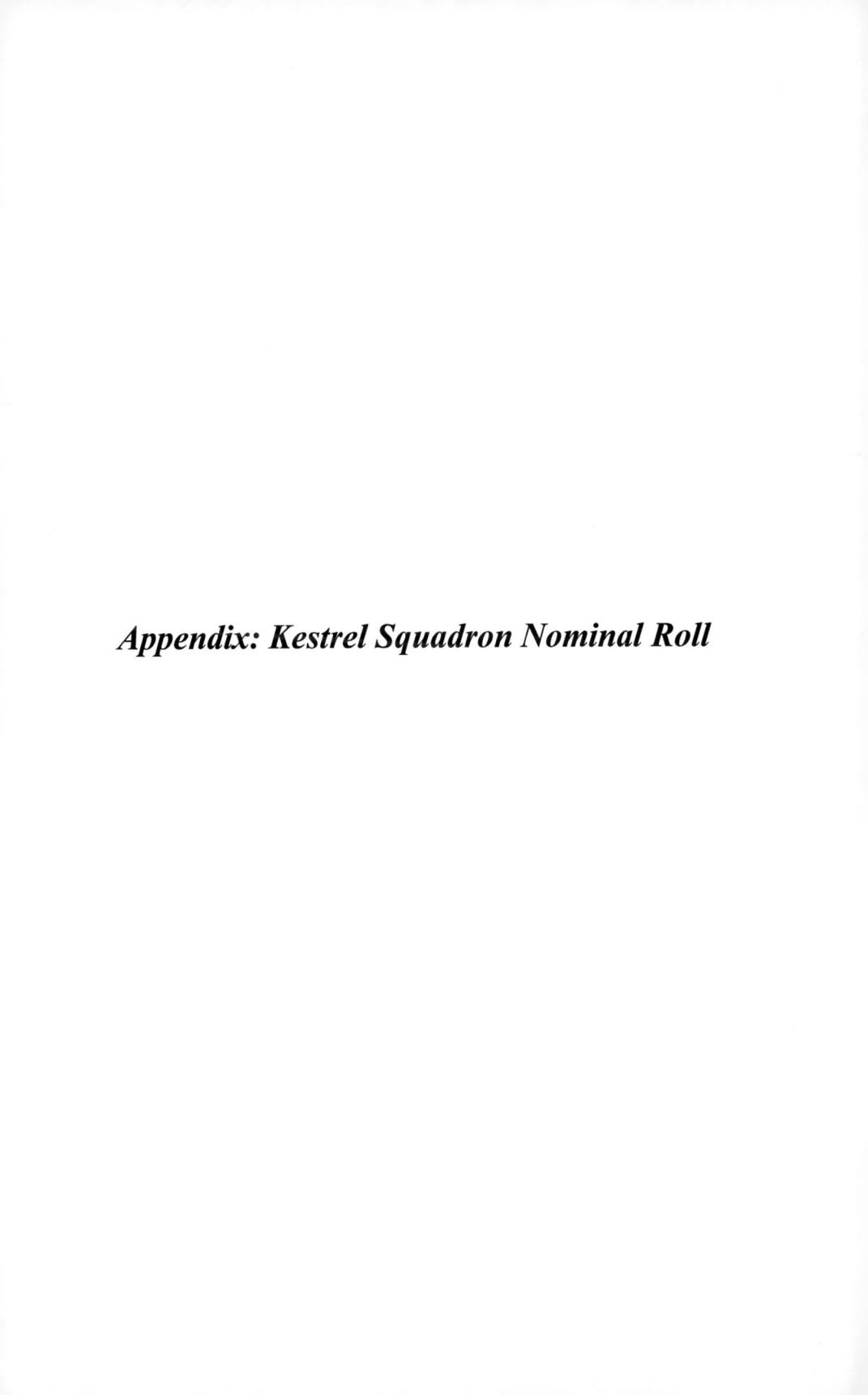

Appendix: Kestrel Squadron Nominal Roll

OFFICERS

Service	Assignment	Rank	Name
Wing Commander	D. McL Scrimgeour	RAF	Officer Commanding/Pilot
Squadron Leader	T.J. D'E Burke	RAF	Senior Technical Officer
Squadron Leader	F.A. Trowern	RAF	Pilot
Flight Lieutenant	D.J. McL. Edmonston	RAF	Pilot
Flight Lieutenant	R.J. Grose	RAF	Sqdn. Adjutant
Flight Lieutenant	R.V.A. Munro	RAF	Pilot
Flying Officer	A.G. Dale	RAF	Photographer Officer
Flying Officer	H.C. Hemsley	RAF	Sqdn. Liaison Officer
Major	A. Campbell	UK ARMY	Army Liaison Officer
Commander	J.J. Tyson	US NAVY	Dep. Officer Commanding/Pilot
Lt. Cl.	L. Solt	US ARMY	Pilot (until April 1965)
Major	P.R. Curry	US ARMY	Pilot (Replaced Lt. Col. Solt)
Major	J.A. Johnston	US ARMY	Pilot
Major	W.W. King	US ARMY	Engineering Officer
Major	J.K. Campbell	USAF	Pilot
Colonel	G.F. Barkhorn	GAF	Dep. Officer Commanding/Pilot
1st Lieutenant	V. Suhr	GAF	Pilot
Hauptman	J. Duskow	GAF	Electrical Officer

ENLISTED/OTHER RANKS

RAF

Rank	Initials	Surname	Trade
Warrant Officer	L.R.	Grover	Aircraft Fitter
Flight Sergeant	R.A.	Angel	Aircraft Fitter
Chief Technician	J.	Riley	Airframe Fitter
Sergeant	D.D.	Grunwell	Airframe Fitter
Sergeant	P.	Smith	Airframe Fitter
Sergeant	D.L.	Boniface	Airframe Fitter
Corporal	A.J.	Ralphs	Airframe Fitter
Corporal	M.J.	Oliver	Airframe Fitter
Corporal	W.J	Giles	Airframe Fitter
Chief Technician	F.	Burrows	Engine Fitter
Sergeant	D.E.	Money	Engine Fitter
Sergeant	B.	Bassett	Engine Fitter
Sergeant	A.W.	Dunham	Engine Fitter
Sergeant	T.	Cresswell	Engine Fitter
Sergeant	F.T.	Russell	Engine Fitter
Sergeant	R.B.C.	Abbott	Engine Fitter
Corporal	P.M.	May	Engine Fitter
Corporal	J.O.R.	Smith	Engine Fitter
Sergeant	A.P.	Rabjohn	Air Radio Fitter
Sergeant	W.H.	Orton	Air Radio Fitter
Sergeant	R.E	Browne	Air Wireless Fitter
Corporal	J.P.	Blake	Air Wireless Fitter
Corporal	T.	Hyland	Air Wireless Fitter

ENLISTED/OTHER RANKS (Continued)

RAF

Rank	Initials	Surname	Trade
Corporal	C.J.	Hannan-Bobe	Air Wireless Fitter
Junior Technician	J.	Temple	Air Wireless Fitter.
Corporal	A.G.	Moir	Grd. Wireless Fitt.
Corporal	J.M.	Hanbrook	Grd. Wireless Fitt.
Chief Technician	C.E.	Henry	Armament Fitter
Chief Technician	W.H.	Philpott	Armament Fitter
Sergeant	D.L.	Middleton	Armament Fitter
Corporal	K.W.	Bennett	Armament Fitter
Corporal	C.B.	Gibbs	Armament Fitter
Sergeant	P.J.	Callaghan	Armament Fitter
Senior Aircraftman	G.C.	Javens	Armament Mech.
Chief Technician	G.C.	Meek	Electrical Fitter
Chief Technician	J.E.	Brooke	Elec. Fitt. (Air)
Corporal	C.	Cox	Elec. Fitt. (Air)
Corporal	B.	Carlin	Elec. Fitt. (Air)
Junior Technician	D.	Thornley	Elec. Fitt. (Air)
Sergeant	A.	Cave	Elec. Fitt. (Grnd.)
Corporal	J.L.	Wells	Elec. Fitt. (Grnd.)
Junior Technician	E.	Greatorex	Elec. Fitt. (Grnd.)
Junior Technician	S.V.	Hunter	Elec. Fitt. (Grnd.)
Senior Aircraftman	D.A.	Davies	Elec. Mech (Grnd.)
Sergeant	E.H.	Rothwell	Instr. Fitter
Sergeant	D.J.	Crouch	Instr. Fitter (Gen)

ENLISTED/OTHER RANKS (Continued)

RAF

Rank	Initials	Surname	Trade
Corporal	R.R.	Chenery	Instrument Fitter (Gen)
Chief Technician	B.W.	Payne	Instrument Fitter (Nav)
Corporal	M.J.	Atkins	Instrument Fitter (Nav)
Junior Technician	J.A.	Thompson	Instrument Fitter (Nav)
Sergeant	G.A.	Christie	Asst. Air Traffic Control
Sergeant	G.R.	McFarland	Asst. Air Traffic Control
Senior Aircraftman	R.A.	Atkinson	Wireless Operator
Senior Aircraftman	A.	Montgomery	Wireless Operator
Senior Aircraftman	B.N.	Reynolds	Wireless Operator
Senior Aircraftman	T.L.	Howell	Telegraphist
Corporal	V.	Collings	Safety Equipment Worker
Corporal	B.D.	Goodwin	Photographer
Corporal	A.D.	Reeves	Photographer
Senior Aircraftman	D.J.	Finlay	Photographer
Senior Aircraftman	J.A.	Stevenson	Photographer
Senior Aircraftman	M.	Walker	Photographer
Leading Aircraftman	W.	Horne	Photographer
Sergeant	H.E.	Wright	Clerk Secretarial
Senior Aircraftman	H.	McTrusty	Clerk Secretarial
Senior Aircraftman	D.	Stewart	Clerk Secretarial
Senior Aircraftman	R.J.	Wilton	Clerk Secretarial
Junior Technician	K.H.	Churcher	Clerk Secretarial Q-Sec-S
Junior Technician	S.C.	McKay	Clerk Secretarial Q-Sec-S

ENLISTED/OTHER RANKS (Continued)

RAF

Senior Aircraftman	A.	Oliver	Typist
Senior Aircraftman	J.	McLean	Clerk Personnel
Corporal	A.G.	Bartlett	Clerk Statistical.
Sergeant	M.	Chiverton	Supplier General
Junior Technician	D.C.	King	Supplier General

US NAVY

Snr. Chf. Petty Officer	R.W.	Roby	Electrical & Instrument Fitter
Chief Petty Officer	D.B.	Lynn	Airframe Fitter
Chief Petty Officer	C.F.	Mouton	Electrical & Instrument Fitter
Petty Officer/1	J.	Bremner	Photographer
Petty Officer/1	M.	Farney	Engine Fitter.
Petty Officer/1	J.	Staffanson	Engine Fitter.
Petty Officer/2	A.C.	De Fazio	Air Wireless Fitter
Petty Officer/2	D.	Johnson	Airframe Fitter
Petty Officer/2	A.M.	Lucero	Airframe Fitter
Petty Officer/2	J.A.	Osbourn	Airframe Fitter

ENLISTED/OTHER RANKS (Continued)

US ARMY

Rank	Initials	Surname	Trade
Master Sergeant	K.N.	Jones	Airframe/Eng. Fitter
Master Sergeant	R.A.	Dix	Airframe Fitter
Sergeant/1	C.A.	Perry	Air Traffic Control
Staff Sergeant	W.H.	Elliott	Armament Fitter
Staff Sergeant	G.A.	Minor	Clerk Admin.
Specialist 6	J.R.	Crupi	Airframe Fitter
Specialist 6	L.G.	Hill	Electrical Fitter
Specialist 5	G.E.	Adair	Airframe Fitter
Specialist 5	C.B.	Canady	Photographer
Specialist 5	C.L.	Darus	Electrical Fitter
Specialist 5	M.R.	Davis	Engine Fit.
Specialist 5	G.C.	Gibson	Instrument Fitter
Specialist 5	H.E.	Pettiford	Instrument Fitter
Specialist 5	R.S.	Steiner	Engine Fitter
Specialist 5	J.H.	Surbrook	Engine Fitter

US ARMY HELICOPTER CREW

Rank	Initials	Surname
CW03	E.E.	Brabec
Specialist 5	R.L.	Eldridge

ENLISTED/OTHER RANKS (Continued)

US AIR FORCE

Senior Master Sergeant	G.T.	Irgens	Instrument Fitter
Senior Master Sergeant	J.W.	Prines	Engine Fitter.
Master Sergeant	B.N.	Arbuckle	Electrical Fitter
Master Sergeant	W.B.	Heim	Airframe Fitter
Tech. Sergeant	C.G.	Massey	Airframe Fitter
Tech. Sergeant	W.G.	Pinto	Airframe Fitter
Tech. Sergeant	H.L.	West	Engine Fitter
Staff Sergeant	E.L.	Burn	Instrument Fitter
Staff Sergeant	A.D.	Snyder	Electrical Fitter
Staff Sergeant	A.L.	Stewart	Engine Fitter

GERMAN AIR FORCE

Stuffz.	H.J.	Scheding	Engine Fitter
Feldwebel	G.	Findiesen	Engine Fitter
Feldwebel	H.D.	Zinndorf	Airframe Fitt

ENLISTED/OTHER RANKS (Continued)

CENTRAL SERVICING DEVELOPMENT ESTABLISHMENT

Rank	Initials	Surname	Trade
Sergeant	A.E.	Fisk	Engine Fitter.
Corporal	J.R.L.	Skinner	Clerk Prog.
Corporal	J.	Williams	Clerk Stats.
Senior Aircraftman	M.J.	Bradbury	Clerk Stats.
Senior Aircraftman	D.L.	Brough	Clerk Prog.
Senior Aircraftman	A.R.	Marshall	Clerk Prog.

A.C. SQUADRON

Rank	Initials	Surname	Trade
Corporal	G.	Robins	Works Sup.

MECHANICAL TRANSPORT

Rank	Initials	Surname	Trade
Corporal	G.	Hodgson	Driver
Corporal		Kitney	Driver
Corporal	G.C.	Rollins	Driver
Senior Aircraftman	A.	Austin	Driver
Senior Aircraftman	R.J.	Bennett	Driver
Senior Aircraftman	J.	Britland	Driver
Senior Aircraftman	J.J.	Corris	Driver
Senior Aircraftman	C.	Murphy	Driver
Senior Aircraftman	R.	Stephenson	Driver
Senior Aircraftman	R.A.	Tolley	Driver

CIVILIANS

Hawker Siddeley Aircraft Ltd.

R.J.	Anton	Representative
A.W.	Black	Representative
P.A.	Noyce	Representative
R.	Fairchild	Flight Test Eng.
A.	Gettings	Flight Test Eng.
C.H.	Phillips	Flight Test Eng.
A.W.	Bedford	Test Pilot
H.C.H	Merewether	Test Pilot
D.	Simpson	Test Pilot

Bristol Siddeley Engines Ltd.

A.	Ankers	Representative
G.W.	Carr	Representative
F.W.	Leech	Representative

Dowty Fuel Systems Ltd.

T.J.	Phillips	Representative

Trials Cell

M.	Hindley-Maggs	MOD Scientific staff
G.	Patterson	U.S. Member
K.	Phillips	F.R.G. Member
F.	Smolenski	F.R.G. Member

Printed by Amazon Italia Logistica S.r.l.
Torrazza Piemonte (TO), Italy